Experiments in Virtual Reality

Acknowledgements

I would like to thank my students T.F. Chiu, Pete Ashcroft, Andrew Wallace and particularly Sam Ellis, for their contributions to this book. In addition, our grateful thanks is extended to the following who gave permission to reproduce photographs:

Virtuality Entertainment Ltd, Leicester, UK
Polhemus Inc.
Stereographics Corporation
Catherine Ikam
Gail Jeffries
Kai Leibrandt
British Gas plc

Experiments in Virtual Reality

DAVID HARRISON
MARK JAQUES

Butterworth-Heinemann
Linacre House, Jordan Hill, Oxford OX2 8DP
A division of Reed Educational and Professional Publishing Ltd

℞ A member of the Reed Elsevier plc group

OXFORD BOSTON JOHANNESBURG
MELBOURNE NEW DELHI SINGAPORE

First published 1996

British Library Cataloguing in Publication Data

A catalogue record for this book is available from the British Library.

ISBN 0 7506 2225 3

Composition and design by ReadyText, Bath

Printed and bound in Great Britain by Scotprint Ltd, Musselburgh

Contents

5   Into 3D   57

6   Physical modelling   77

Preface

The software given with this book is intended to demonstrate the principles which underlie virtual reality. It was not our intention to produce a commercial virtual reality software package. Instead we set out to provide open code, running under DOS and *Windows*, which can be incorporated into your own programs. The software should be treated as algorithms which describe a particular VR principle. These algorithms should be rewritten in the software language of your choice.

David Harrison
Mark Jaques

Chapter 1

Defining virtual reality

'The ultimate display would be a room within which the computer can control the existence of matter. A chair displayed in such a room would be good enough to sit in. Handcuffs displayed in such a room would be confining, and a bullet displayed in such a room would be fatal. With appropriate programming such a display could literally be the wonderland in which Alice walked.'

Ivan Sutherland

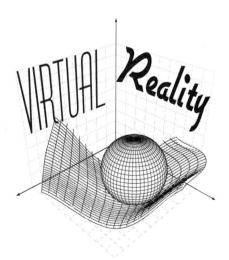

What is VR?

Is it: *a computer-generated, interactive three dimensional environment in which a person is immersed?* There are as many definitions of virtual reality (VR) as there are companies trying to sell systems. However, a useful definition is: *virtual reality is the delivery to a human of the most convincing illusion possible that they are in another reality.* This reality exists in digital electronic form in the memory of a computer.

VR is a way for humans to visualise, manipulate and interact with computers. Instead of using screens and keyboards, helmets with small screens project pictures in front of the users eyes, and 'datagloves' transmit the movements of the users hand to the computer. Movement of the head may be sensed and the view on the screens appropriately modified, enabling one to 'look around' the world. A user can move about, pick-up and interact with objects within this world. The experience of being connected to all this technology should, ideally, be close to entering another world. However, the truth is a little different.

Figure 1.1
Retinal image

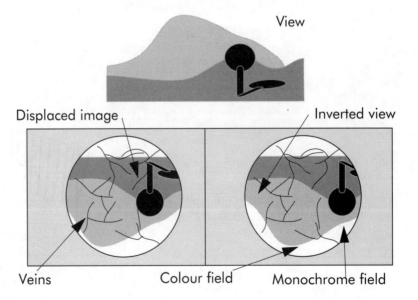

The majority of virtual realities created so far are extremely crude and expensive. They generally look like video games and are slow to react. Computers today just aren't powerful enough to generate anything near 'reality'. However, humans have immense powers of imagination, and do not need a perfect simulation to come to believe that it is some form of reality. Figure 1.1 shows the image the eye actually receives at the retina and gives an idea of the visual processing capabilities of the human brain. Perception is a cognitive process not a purely optical process – ie the brain 'sees': two displaced images which are inverted; veins; a central colour field and an outer monochrome field. From this image the brain constructs a model of the world which we call reality. VR systems are already being developed for applications as diverse as robot operation in hazardous situations, molecular manipulation for drug design, surgical training and metrology.

Immersion and desktop VR systems

In an 'immersive' virtual environment the user is presented with computer-generated views using displays – generally mounted on the head – that prevent sensory data from physical reality from reaching the person's senses. This contrasts with 'desktop' systems where the user views a standard computer monitor display from a normal distance. Desktop systems are generally more widely used, principally due to the higher costs and problems of fatigue and motion sickness which have been associated with head-mounted displays. However, for the purists, immersion *is* VR.

Immersion can lead to a sense of presence, a state of consciousness where the user has the sense of being in the location specified by the displays. The level of presence will vary significantly between individuals; for one particular individual, excellent graphics without sound may be enough to generate a strong feeling of presence but for another a fairly abstract display, such as a 'wireframe' would be sufficient if coupled with 3D audio information. Researchers investigating 'presence' in VR classify it as an experience which is more like 'visiting a place' than 'seeing images' of a place. The user should, in this state, experience objects and processes in the virtual world as temporarily more 'real' than the outside physical world. As a result of this the user should exhibit reactions like those they would produce in similar circumstances – duck when passing under virtual objects, hesitate at the top of steps, etc.

Our view of the outside world comes from a vast stream of sensory information: vision, hearing, touch and smell. Closely coupled with this is our view of where we are, derived from signals from our muscles and our joints: known as *proprioceptive* data. To render a 'fully immersive' experience it is not enough to provide a display system that inputs visual, sound, touch and smell data directly into human sensory systems. The *human body itself* must be tracked so that changes in the displays are driven by movements of the human body.

Thus, ideally, the turning of the head is tracked and relayed to the computer system, which causes appropriate changes in the computer displays. Ideally, these changes are matched to the internally-generated muscle and joint signals which tell the viewer they have turned their head. Unfortunately, even the most advanced of today's VR systems fails to meet this goal. Generally, there is a *lag* caused by the system's communication and computation needs, which results in a mismatch between what the display shows and what the feedback from the user's muscles and joints tells him. It is thought that this lag may be one of the major factors in the motion sickness problems associated with immersive VR.

A brief history of VR

Virtual reality has its roots in simulation, (particularly flight simulation), computer graphics and computer arcade games – so it's difficult to set an exact start date for VR.

The early flight simulators

Flight simulators date back to 1910 and were aimed at training pilots quickly, cheaply and safely. The Link Trainer, Figure 1.2, developed in the 1920s, used pneumatics to reproduce aircraft movement, and had a cockpit that rolled and pitched in response to control movements. However, its technology could not produce a faithful simulation of flight. It was not until the development of the electronic computer in the 1950s that simulators could be built around mathematical equations which modelled the characteristics of flight. By using a computer the numbers displayed on the pilot's instrument panels – the airspeed, the height, and the heading – could represent the effect of the pilot's control movements on the aircraft.

Figure 1.2 The Link Trainer

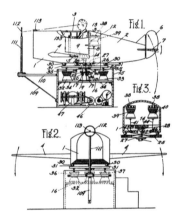

The Sensorama

Around the time when electronic computers were first being used for flight simulation, an interesting 'immersive' machine was produced by Morton Heilig, aimed at the entertainment industry.

Figure 1.3 The Sensorama ride

Called *The Sensorama* (see Figure 1.3) it took the user on virtual bicycle rides through Brooklyn and Californian sand dunes using 3D film clips, vibrating handlebars and seat, and the smell of pizza and exhaust fumes to create an 'artificial reality'. Sadly, the machine was never mass produced.

Ivan Sutherland and 'The Ultimate Display'

Many credit Ivan Sutherland's 1965 paper, *The ultimate display*, as being the kick-off point for virtual reality. In this paper Sutherland proposed the idea of generalised simulation, with an interface that could produce the experience of being in an artificial space 'within which the computer can control the existence of matter'. He followed this in 1968 with *A head-mounted three dimensional display* which outlined work he had carried out at Harvard on a 3D helmet display, and a tracking sensor. The helmet used two miniature TV screens mounted in front of the eyes. The tracking sensor monitored position and movement of the user. Two approaches were tried for this: one, *The Sword of Damocles*, used an adjustable rod extending from the ceiling to the helmet to track head position. The second approach used an ultrasonic source mounted on the helmet giving more freedom and a larger range.

Sutherland's idea was to simulate 'looking around' models of 3D objects. Tracking the helmet's position, the computers would work out the appropriate appearance of objects and display them to the user. The objects would be made bigger and smaller as the user moves, and changes in the user's viewing angle would change the perspective. Sutherland also proposed that physical laws such as gravity could be applied to the objects, allowing them to respond naturally. These ideas are still central to what is known as virtual reality and examples of these techniques are explored later in the book.

Many of the key developments envisaged by Sutherland occurred in the 1980s, through such defence initiatives as the *Supercockpit Project* based at the Wright Patterson Air Force Base in Dayton, Ohio; and through efforts in telepresence and robot control at the NASA Ames Research Centre in California. The 1980s brought technological improvements in three areas critical to VR development: liquid crystal display and cathode ray tube technology for displays, image generation systems, and tracking systems for converting position and orientation data. The NASA Ames research centre lead VR research through the 1980s, developing a wide angle, head-mounted stereoscopic display system called VIEW, which was controlled by the subject's position and gestures. Lightweight LCD displays replaced the cathode ray tubes used by Sutherland, and the mechanical tracker was replaced by electronic sensors, but the head- mounted display was in principle similar to Sutherland's original.

The aim of this book

The aim of this book is to introduce those with some computing experience to the equipment and software techniques behind virtual reality systems. The best systems around still cost millions, budget systems can be had for thousands. This book aims to show you how to put together a system that illustrates the principles of VR, and educates in a practical way, for around £100. The book shows how simple dataglove and tracker devices may be built up using very basic electronic hardware and computer software. The building of 'virtual worlds' – graphical computer environments which can be controlled using the glove and tracker, is also covered. After reading the text, experimenting with the programs and building and interfacing some of the input devices, the reader should have a good grounding in the subject.

The importance of VR

Virtual reality is a key technological growth area of the future with many applications, including: entertainment, product design and visualisation, architecture, molecular modelling and surgery. A grounding in the principles and practical application of virtual reality will give the reader a competitive advantage in many fields.

The elements of VR

There are three parts to a typical VR system. Firstly, the visual, tactile and acoustic sub-systems through which the user sees, feels and hears the virtual world. Secondly, the manual controls for navigating through

the virtual world. This can be as simple as a joystick but more sophisti-
cated systems provide a glove containing position sensors for the hand
or even a suit that covers the entire body. Finally, there are central
coordinating processors and software. Figure 1.4 shows the system
architecture of a virtual reality system.

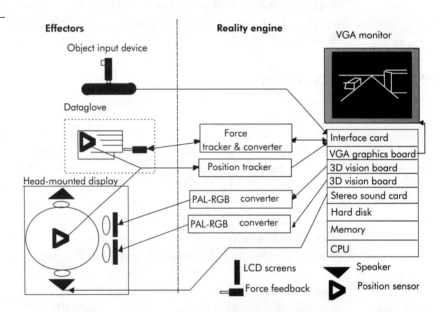

Figure 1.4 VR system architecture

Together, these can be used to navigate through 3D environments and
experience visiting a world that would be physically impossible in our
own reality – the world you see is virtual, it exists only in the computer
and in the equipment you are wearing. From the user's point of view, a
virtual reality system consists of three main 'experiences': manipulation,
navigation and immersion.

- ▸ **Manipulation:** the ability to reach out, touch and move objects
  in the virtual world.

- ▸ **Navigation:** the ability to move about and explore the virtual
  world.

- ▸ **Immersion:** is about completely enclosing the user, using head-
  mounted displays which fill the field of view, as well as providing
  audio and tactile information.

System builders who are trying to deliver this 'VR experience' have a very different view of VR. From their point of view, VR presents three key tasks:

▸ **Sensing of the real environment:** sensing head, hand, and/or body position and attitude of the participant.

▸ **Control of the virtual environment:** based on the acquired sensor information, the characteristics and behaviour of objects within the environment are controlled.

▸ **Display of the virtual environment:** this involves not only visual aspects of the environment, but may also include sound, and perhaps tactile feedback displays.

Figure 1.5 VR sub-systems

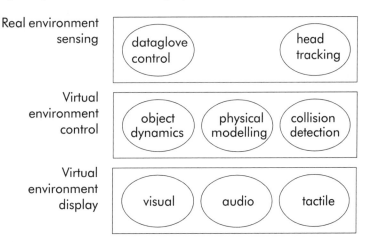

Real environment sensing

- dataglove control
- head tracking

Virtual environment control

- object dynamics
- physical modelling
- collision detection

Virtual environment display

- visual
- audio
- tactile

In this book, the construction of hardware is followed by the development of the necessary mathematical and graphical software required to demonstrate the appropriate VR principles. We make a start with 'sensing'. Chapter 2 describes how to construct and then interface a dataglove to your PC. In Chapter 3 a kinematic model of the hand is developed and this model is displayed as a 3D image. Chapter 4 covers the development of ultrasonic and mechanical tracking devices.

Control of the virtual environment

Chapter 5 covers the construction of a virtual environment containing objects to manipulate. The behaviour of the objects is controlled by equations which simulate the behaviour of their real-world counter-parts. A pair of stereo glasses and some clever software can convey something of the feel of true 'immersion'.

Physical modelling

A physical model of object behaviour is developed in Chapter 6 which allows the user to deform material through manipulation. This physical model also provides force-feedback data which could be used to constrain the movement of a glove to give the user the impression that the material is resisting deformation.

VR applications

In Chapter 7 we look at a number of applications of VR principles.

Chapter 2

DIY datagloves

A dataglove is a glove fitted with sensors to measure the positions of the user's fingers. Once connected to a computer, the glove may be used to communicate with a computer using simple gestures. A user can, for example, grab an object in a virtual world and move it about. This is a simple and natural way to interact with a computer, using the innate capabilities of our senses to achieve insights not possible with other methods. The best way to learn about datagloves is probably to build one. However, the patent law covering datagloves is complex and we do not wish to be seen to be 'inciting' you to make gloves in breach of patent. Nevertheless, a number of gloves have been made successfully as student projects and we report on the features of these DIY designs. We start by surveying commercial gloves.

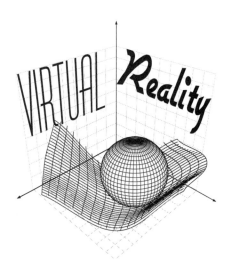

A survey of gloves

There are numerous input devices on the market. These include gloves, wands, 'flying mice' and 'force balls'. Not all of them detect finger positions, but all that deserve a mention are described below.

The VPL dataglove

This is the best known of the gloves. It is a wired clothing device that uses fibre optic loops that measure the amount of bend or flex of a body joint. These work because, as a fibre bends, the amount of light passing through it is reduced. This is picked up by a sensor and processed.

Figure 2.1
The VPL
dataglove

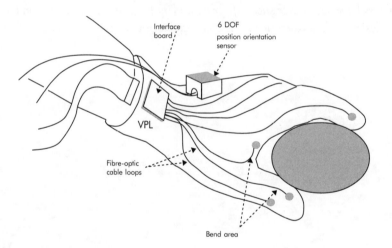

The glove construction
The fibre optic cables pass over the palm and finger joints. The fibre optic cable is specially designed so that when it is bent light escapes. Each cable has a light-emitting diode at one end and a phototransistor at the other. The more light is lost the greater the movement. The phototransistors convert the light into an electrical signal. This signal is scanned by a microprocessor in the glove which calculates the angle of the joints by using a known model of the hand. The glove measures 16 angles on the hand. This glove uses an RS-232 serial port, which makes it compatible with most computers.

Mattel Power Glove

This was the only virtual reality (VR) product that was mass produced: developed for the Nintendo computer game system. During the year that it was available tens of thousands of the gloves were bought.

Figure 2.2
The Power
Glove

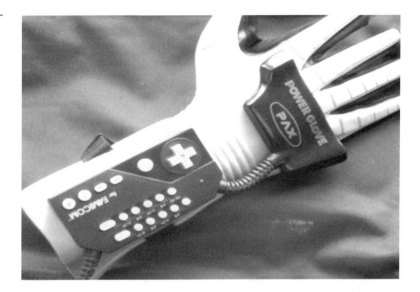

It works by using conductive ink on a strip of plastic inside each finger of the glove; when the fingers were bent the resistance of the ink changed. It was sold at $89, a much cheaper device than the VPL glove (which it was based on) but it was nowhere near as accurate. An analogue-to-digital convertor was used to read the sensors, and an 8-bit processor monitors the fingers and communicates with the host computer. This glove used an ultrasonic position and orientation sensor.

Sarcos Exoskeletal Hand Master

This glove uses mechanical links over each joint to determine the angle of that joint. The measurement is by Hall effect sensors and magnets built into the hinge assembly: as the hinge moves so does the magnet, and therefore the voltage changes in the sensor. The result is very accurate and repeatable measurements, but its bulkiness limits its use in some applications. The cost of one glove with 20 sensors is $15,000.

The Hand Master connects to any AT-bus PC compatible through a custom data-acquisition board. This glove is more precise than the fibre optic glove as it has sensors for all the joints of the finger and makes no assumptions. It also has extra sensors for side-to-side movements of the fingers and thumb.

Figure 2.3
Six degrees
of freedom
of an object

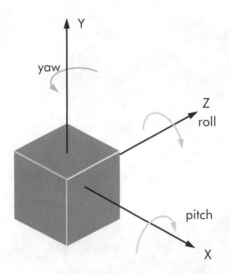

Wands and flying mice

Wands are very simple, consisting of a 6 DOF (Degrees Of Freedom) sensor and a couple of switches. Unconstrained objects have six different directions or rotations they can move in. Objects can move along any of the three axes (X, Y, Z) and can rotate about any of these principal axes. All together they add up to six different degrees of freedom in which an object can move.

Because of this simplicity they are very easy to use. They are akin to flying mice. Flying mice are similar to normal 2D mice, except they have a 6 DOF sensor attached – usually a *Polhemus*.

Biological input sensors

Someday the need to wear a wired glove may be eliminated. Instead of a glove, a simple tight-fitting bracelet might be able to distinguish between individual finger movements. It might work by detecting the small electronic signal from muscles when they move, or by the movement of the tendons in the wrist. There is already a prototype system that lets a user travel through a virtual world, by eye movement: when the eye muscles move, a dermal sensor picks up the electrical signals they generate.

DIY glove design

For a DIY dataglove you need a device that will reliably:

- input data from movements of the hand
- display these in real time
- recognise gestures made by the user.

and achieve all of this on a very limited budget. The design of the glove and gesture input system can be split into three parts:

- sensor design
- glove design
- circuit design.

Sensor design

The sensors that determine the amount the fingers bend must be:

- durable
- inexpensive
- easily maintainable
- accurate
- possible to be made with off-the-shelf parts.

To be easily interfaced to a computer, the sensors must give a change of voltage when the angle of the finger joints are changed.

Possible methods for finger angle detection are: potentiometers, strain gauges, skin resistance, pressure sensing, piezo-electric wire, optic fibres or light tubes.

Any of these approaches could be used successfully to construct a glove. The potentiometer and light tube approaches are perhaps the easiest to use on a limited budget.

Potentiometers

It is possible to construct a glove using a miniature rotary potentiometer fixed over the first joint of each finger, see Figure 2.4.

When the finger is bent the armature rotates, which in turn rotates the potentiometer. This gives a change in resistance which may be used to determine the finger angle. This design works though it is rather uncomfortable to wear and it is difficult to develop a sturdy and reliable glove using these sensors.

Figure 2.4
Potentio-
meter design

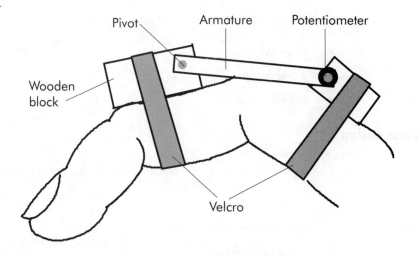

Gloves have also been made sucessfully using linear potentiometers or 'sliders'. A string attached to the tip of the finger moves the potentiometer in response to finger flexure and a spring returns the potentiometer slider to its starting postion when the finger is straightened.

Optic fibres

Many existing gloves use optic fibres in their construction. Fibres have been developed with a special coating which enables the amount they are bent to be measured; however, these are not generally available.

Figure 2.5
The final
sensor
design

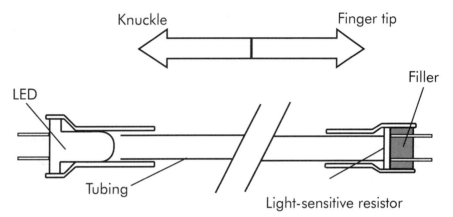

If the outer coating of a normal fibre is removed and the surface slightly roughened the same effect can be seen. However, the fibres tend to break after repeated use and much patient work with a file is needed to produce the right effect.

Light tube

An alternative is to use the effect that when a small tube is bent, the amount of light which travels from one end to the other is reduced. A slim black plastic tube is placed along each of the fingers and the thumb, over the knuckle and finger joints. A light-emitting diode is placed at one end and a photosensitive resistor at the other, shown in Figure 2.5. When a finger, and therefore tube, is bent, the amount of light reaching the sensor at the end of the tube is reduced and the output from the sensor changes. One of the great advantages over the potentiometer approach is that there are no moving parts to fail. The sensor is extremely sensitive to even the smallest amount of external light, so steps must be taken to exclude unwanted light. Heat-stuck plastic sleeving may be used to seal the sensor and LED onto the tube ends. This design is extremely cheap (one sensor costs about £1 with off-the-shelf components), extremely simple, all the components are easily available and the circuit requires no amplifiers.

Circuit design

The circuit for one sensor is shown in Figure 2.6. It consists of the LED, with a series resistor to limit the current through it, and a voltage divider. The divider has the light-dependent resistor on one side and a resistor chosen to give the greatest voltage change for the sensor to travel from dark to full light. An analogue-to-digital convertor is needed to read the voltage across the sensor. Whenever possible ribbon cables and connectors should be used, to keep the glove system tidy and manageable.

Figure 2.6 A circuit for 1 sensor

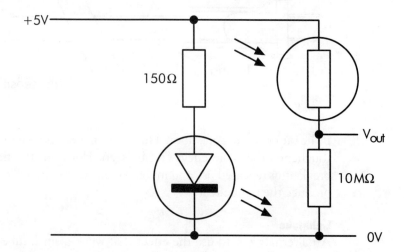

Glove construction

For the light-pipe glove, the glove construction was based on a tight black cloth glove (bought from M&S), with cloth tubes stuck on each of the fingers – down which the sensor assembly is pushed, (parts list in Appendix B). A plug and socket connector was used at the wrist to connect the individual wires from the sensors to a neat strip of ribbon cable which connects to the computer interface board. Whichever sensor technique you decide to use, it is best to start by making up just one sensor, attaching it to a glove, and checking that you can measure the sensor voltage on your computer. Once you have got one sensor working, it is a simple matter to repeat the process for three more fingers and a thumb.

Figure 2.7
First
prototype
glove

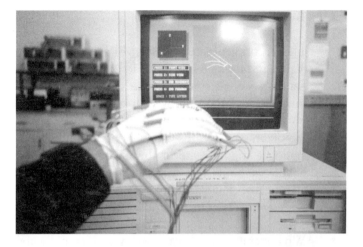

Figure 2.8
Final glove
design

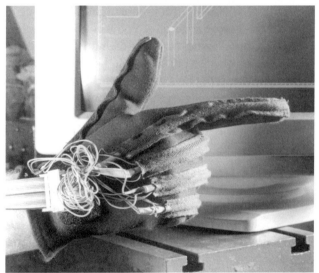

If you have problems measuring the varying sensor voltage with your computer, use a meter to check that the sensor voltage varies as you bend and straighten the sensor. If it does not, then check each of your connections carefully, and try again.

Interfacing the glove

The sensors generate analogue voltages which must be converted into a digital form which can be read and processed by a computer. Many computers come complete with an A–D port, but you must ensure that the voltages produced by your glove sensors are compatible with the port. The IBM PC has no A–D conversion or port as standard. However, games cards can be bought quite cheaply which do provide analogue inputs. One of the cheapest analogue-to-digital convertor boards we could find was the *Roldec A/D* board for the PC, with 16 channels of analogue input for around £50. Roldec's address and phone number are given in Appendix B.

Whatever interface board you choose, a rapidly updated measure of the analogue voltage on the sensor should be placed in a specific memory location of your computer. You will need a short test program to take the measured values from this memory location and display them to the screen, to check your board and glove operation. You should get a suitable test program supported with your board. Once you can waggle the fingers of your glove and some numbers on the screen change, you will need to calibrate your glove. If you are using a *Roldec* A/D board you can simply run program VR'V5-31 on the accompanying disk: you will be asked to calibrate the glove.

> **Note:** if you do not use the *Roldec* board then the addresses used by your interface card may differ from those used in our software. You will have to replace the addresses in the open *QuickBasic* version of the program with the appropriate ones for your board.

Calibration

For the computer to use the sensor voltages they must be converted into another form, here we have converted them to degrees, with 0° as the hand being flat and 90° fully clenched. The subroutine calibrate first initialises the calibration by inputting and storing the voltage when the hand is fully bent and flat. A second subroutine takes each reading from the glove and converts it to an angle. The calibration routine matches the range of voltage variation between clenched and open fingers with the appropriate movement on the screen.

Uses of datagloves

Sign language recognition

An interesting first application for the glove is sign language translation. Research workers at Stanford University in the USA developed a 'Talking Glove' for the deaf–blind, which recognised American sign language (see Figure 2.9), and used a speech synthesizer to speak the signed letters. Using the code on the disk your glove may be easily programmed to recognise American sign language and print the appropriate letters to the screen. If you want to extend the system to include speech synthesis, well, we'll leave that up to you.

Figure 2.9
American sign language

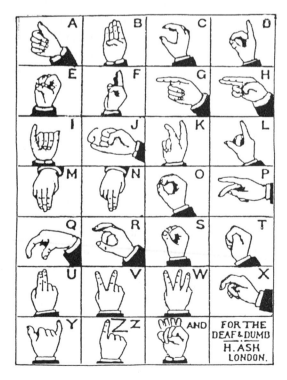

To use the pattern-recognition software, copy the contents of the subdirectory DATAGLOV onto your hard disk in C:\DATAGLOV. If you have built the dataglove, type VR'V5-31. The program will ask you to calibrate the glove, by opening your hand flat then making a fist. Then try making one of the shapes with your hand that are shown in Figure 2.9. Start with something simple like an 'f'. The appropriate letter should be displayed on the bottom of your computer's screen.

If you have not built the glove you may still be interested in seeing the computer 'hand model' stepping through the sign language alphabet. To do this, enter the DATAGLOV directory and type VR-NOGLOV, then F for the File menu, O to open a file, then the filename Alphabet. This loads a file of hand poses. Press V for View, and D for Demo, and a demonstration will run, stepping through the sign language alphabet.

A development of the PatternRec routine allows any pose to be programmed into the computer: simply by putting the glove into that pose, and pressing a button. Each of the finger positions is recorded and can be recalled at any time. If the hand is put in that pose the computer can recognise and display the name allocated for the pose. The computer stores each pose in a record which is part of an array. The array can be added to, changed, deleted, loaded from and saved to disk, using the menu system.

An 'air guitar'

You could quite easily extend the PatternRec routine used for sign language recognition to give an 'air guitar'. This is particularly appropriate because the first dataglove was developed by a musician in search of an 'air guitar'. Thousands of rock fans thrash away with empty hands, miming along to favourite tracks. But make up a left-handed glove as described earlier, program your computer to recognise the main guitar chord shapes, and make the right noises, and you can play along with an 'air guitar'. With your guitar you have the disadvantage that unlike a cardboard guitar, you do need to know how to play! Assuming the signals from your glove are calibrated and being read by the computer, all you need is a recognition routine to recognise the chord positions and output the right sounds. The modifications required to the existing pattern routine below are very simple.

The Egyptian fortress of Buhen
(Courtesy of SENSE8™.)

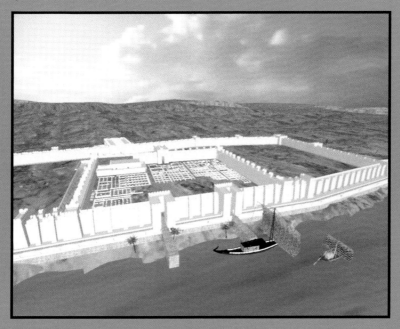

WorldToolKit by Sense8 Corporation was used to create a real-time tour of the ancient Egyptian Fortress of Buhen. William Riseman Associates built the architectural model of this fortification based on detailed archaelogical data provided by the Boston Museum of Fine Arts' Egyptian Department.

The Mars Rover

(Courtesy of SENSE8™ and the NASA Ames Research Center.)

NASA Ames Research Center, McDonnell-Douglas and Sense8 Corporation jointly developed a real-time simulation of the Mars terrain and 1996 Marsicov Rover using WorldToolKit. During the actual NASA Mars mission the database will be dynamically updated based on feedback from the Mars Rover, further refining the simulation. Scientists on earth will have the opportunity to explore the realistic surface of the planet through virtual reality technology.

The
PatternRec
routine

```
SUB PatternRec
COLOR 14
LOCATE 23, 40
PRINT "-";
' CALL FindPattern (Thu%, Ind%, Mid%, Rin%, Lit%, letter)
' 0½ - Fingers Straight, 90½ - Fingers Curled up
CALL FindPattern (0, 90, 90, 90, 90, "A")
CALL FindPattern (0, 0, 0, 0, 0, "B")
CALL FindPattern (25, 25, 25, 25, 25, "C")
CALL FindPattern (35, 0, 35, 35, 35, "D")
CALL FindPattern (0, 70, 0, 0, 0, "F")
CALL FindPattern (0, 0, 70, 70, 70, "G")
CALL FindPattern (0, 70, 70, 70, 0, "I")
CALL FindPattern (0, 0, 20, 70, 70, "P")
CALL FindPattern (0, 35, 70, 70, 70, "Q")
CALL FindPattern (0, 0, 0, 70, 70, "V")
CALL FindPattern (0, 0, 0, 0, 70, "W")
END SUB
SUB FindPattern (T%, I%, M%, R%, L%, letter$)
   ' angle can vary þ a%
   a% = 10
   IF InRange (ANG% (0), T%, a%) AND InRange (ANG%(1), I%, a%) AND
   InRange(ANG%(2),
   PRINT letter$;
   END IF
END SUB
```

Chapter 3

The virtual hand

Now we have a dataglove, what is needed is a means of viewing the information from the glove. This chapter explains how to do this using a 'virtual hand' displayed on the computer screen. The hand is initially a stick model, animated by the movement of the dataglove. It uses the simplest method of drawing a 3D shape, which is a wireframe in which the corners or vertices of the shape are joined together by lines or wires.

We discuss the principles of kinematic modelling and apply these to the construction of a model of the hand produced from individual finger and thumb elements. This model is then used to translate finger flexure measurements from the dataglove and convert these to screen coordinates. Later in this chapter, by viewing translational matrices, we are able to scale, rotate and tilt the model to afford different views of the hand. We conclude by surveying current display technology including head-mounted and head-coupled displays as well as light-weight stereo LCD shutter glasses and full-scale virtual reality rooms.

Kinematic modelling

The basic hand configuration is shown in Figure 3.1. The information about the user's finger positions is translated into the screen co-ordinates using what is known as a *kinematic model*. To draw the hand on the screen the positions of each joint of the finger must be found in 3D space, and lines are drawn to link each joint. Initially, there are six fixed points, the origin and each knuckle. The kinematic model takes the angle of each finger and calculates the joint positions in absolute co-ordinates. This gives the screen co-ordinates when the hand is viewed from the front, without any tilting or spinning of the image. A number of assumptions are made in modelling the hand: it is assumed that when one joint on a finger bends, all the joints on that finger bend by an equivalent amount. This means that the model cannot distinguish between the movement of just one joint and the movement of the whole finger. It is possible to do this, but it requires a separate sensor for each joint. Also, the extra computer time needed to process the data from the additional sensors would make the update time unacceptably high on a PC.

Figure 3.1
Basic hand
model

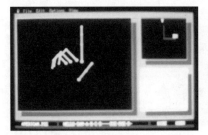 

Calculating the absolute co-ordinates

The reference frame used for these programs is the right-handed co-ordinate set. These co-ordinates are known as right-handed because if the thumb, 1st finger and 2nd finger of the right hand are held at right angles to one another they point in the direction of the X, Y and Z axes. The bend sensor gives a measure of finger flexure, which gives an approximate measure of finger angle to the knuckle joint as shown in Figure 3.2.

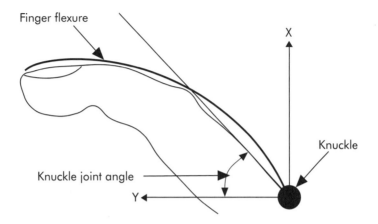

Figure 3.2
Finger flexure to
finger angle

Finger model

As you curl your finger, the joints do not bend by the same amount: clench your right hand and look at the side of the index finger. You can see that knuckle has bent about 90°, but the first joint has bent about 120° and the second about 60°. Assuming that this relationship holds throughout the finger's movement (see Figure 3.3), a bend of θ (theta) for the knuckle would result in bends of $1.3 \times \theta$ and $0.7 \times \theta$ for the first and second joints respectively. It is this trick which allows us to create a very simple and fast model of the hand.

To draw the finger the computer requires the knuckle joint and first and second joint co-ordinates. The system then draws small circles at each joint and joins them with lines to form a representation of finger segments. The finger model joint co-ordinates are calculated trigonometrically after making a number of assumptions discussed in the *Kinematic modelling* section, page 26. The fingers are constrained to move in the X–Y plane, therefore the Z-values for each point for each finger are the same at all times. The position of the knuckle joint is known. From this the position of the first joint can be calculated from the bend angle and the length of the finger segment. Once the position of this joint is known, the next joint can be calculated and so on until the fingertip is reached. The angle, from the vertical, for the segment between the first joint and the second joint will be the sum of the knuckle angles and the first joint angle. The equations are given below.

Figure 3.3 The finger model

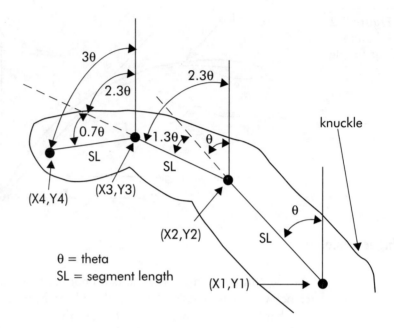

The position of the knuckle is given by:

```
X1 = constant
Y1 = constant
Z1 = Z2 = Z3 = Z4 = constant
```

The middle joint position is given by:

```
X2 = X1 - segment length*SIN(theta)
Y2 = Y1 + segment length*COS(theta)
```

The end joint is given by:

```
X3= X2 - segment length*SIN(2.3*theta)
Y3= Y2 + segment length*COS(2.3*theta)
```

And the finger tip is given by:

```
X4= X3 - segment length*SIN(3*theta)
Y4= Y3 + segment length*COS(3*theta)
```

Modelling the thumb

Modelling the thumb is very similar to that of the finger, except that both the joints bend by theta; the angles do not start at the vertical and the thumb is constrained in the Y–Z plane rather than the X–Y plane. The problem of the starting angle being 45° from the vertical is easily solved by replacing the angle theta by (theta–gama/4), where gama/4 is the starting angle in radians. The equations for the absolute co-ordinates of the thumb are shown below. It can be seen that the Y-equations are unchanged and the Z-equations are equivalent to the X-equations for the fingers.

The knuckle position is given by:

```
X1 = X2 = X3 = X4 = constant
Y1 = constant
Z1 = constant
```

The middle joint is given by:

```
Y2 = Y1 + segment length*COS(theta-gama/4)
Z2 = Z1 - segment length*SIN(theta-gama/4)
```

The thumb end is given by:

```
Y3 = Y2 + segment length*COS(2*theta- gama/4)
Z3 = Z2 - segment length*SIN(2*theta- gama/4)
```

The thumb has only three joints, the fourth being within the hand, thus the redundant fourth co-ordinate is given by:

```
Y4 = Y3
Z4 = Z3
```

A simple program for drawing the hand

The program described in this section has been reduced to the essentials, it merely takes in data about the finger positions, calculates the appropriate screen co-ordinates for the joints from this data (using the above equations), and then draws the joints and the linking lines.

For demonstration purposes we have included some fixed angle positions as data, to save having to connect a glove at this stage. Figure 3.4 shows various hand positions to illustrate the kinematic model.

Figure 3.4
Kinematic
model of hand

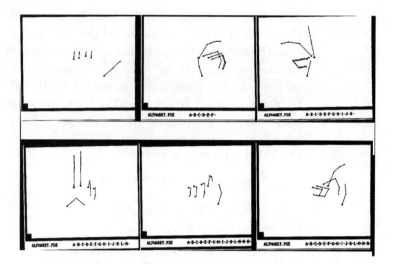

Program explanation

At the core of the program are three subroutine calls, followed by a six-line loop. First the routine Setup is called. This contains the positions of the finger joints and the lengths of the connecting finger segments as shown in Figure 3.5.

Subroutine
Setup

```
SUB Setup
    SCREEN 9, , 1, 1
    COLOR 7, 0
    x1(0) = -30: y1(0) = 0: z1(0) = 30 'Thumb
    x1(1) = 0: y1(1) = 110: z1(1) = 30 'Index
    x1(2) = 0: y1(2) = 115: z1(2) = 10 'Middle
    x1(3) = 0: y1(3) = 110: z1(3) = -14'Ring
    x1(4) = 0: y1(4) = 105: z1(4) = -32'Little
' Finger segment lengths: Knuckle to joint 1
' and joint 1 to joint 2.
    k2j1(1) = 55: j12j2(1) = 32
    k2j1(2) = 60: j12j2(2) = 36
    k2j1(3) = 55: j12j2(3) = 34
    k2j1(4) = 46: j12j2(4) = 27
' The best colours for 3D are bright red, 12, and
' bright green, 10. Use red & blue filters for these
    col% = 12: Lcol% = 4: Rcol% = 2
    apage% = 1: vpage% = 0
    view$ = "SIDE ": type$ = "WIRE "
    Spin% = 40: Tilt% = 350
END SUB
```

Figure 3.5
Initial finger
positions

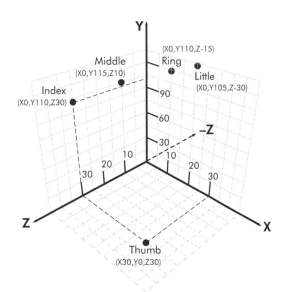

The loop shown below then allows the user to select the appropriate model, wireframe, solid or 3D. We will deal with wireframe here, and consider the other two in later chapters.

Subroutine
Wire

```
SUB Wire
DO
    ANG%(0) = INT(RND*90): ANG%(1) = INT(RND*90): ANG%(2) = INT(RND*90):
    ANG%(3) = INT(RND * 90): ANG%(4) = INT(RND * 90)
        CALL CalcThumb
    CALL CalcFingers
    CLS
    CALL DrawHand
    key$ = INKEY$
    CALL PatternRec
LOOP WHILE key$ = ""
END SUB
```

The Wire routine calls CalcFingers which calculates the world co-ordinates for each joint on each finger, and then converts them to screen co-ordinates. CalcThumb does a similar job for the thumb (the function of the SpinTilt program will be explained in the section *Transformations – spinning and tilting the model*, on page 33).

Subroutine
CalcFingers

```
SUB CalcFingers
' ************************ SUB : CalcFingers *************************
'
' This calculates the x ,y and z WORLD co-ordinates for each joint
' on each of the 4 fingers , then converts them to SCREEN co-ordinates.
' i.e x1, y1 & z1 are the co-ordinates of the point. To convert them to
' screen co-ords they are rotated about the Z-axis (out of screen) then
' about the Y-axis (up). The sx1 & sy1 are then plotted.
'
' ********************************************************************

FOR I% = 1 TO 4
' Convert finger angle to Radians
    theta = (ANG%(I%) * pi) / 180
' Z values are the same for all
    zSpinS = z1(I%) * SpinSin

' The knuckle position is given in data
    sx1(I%) = x1(I%) * SpinCTiltC + y1(I%) * SpinCTiltS - zSpinS
    sy1(I%) = -x1(I%) * TiltSin + y1(I%) * TiltCos

' Calculate the middle joint position
    x2 = x1(I%) - k2j1(I%) * SIN(theta)
    y2 = y1(I%) + k2j1(I%) * COS(theta)
    sx2(I%) = x2 * SpinCTiltC + y2 * SpinCTiltS - zSpinS
    sy2(I%) = -x2 * TiltSin + y2 * TiltCos

' Calculate the end joint position
    x3 = x2 - j12j2(I%) * SIN(2.3 * theta)
    y3 = y2 + j12j2(I%) * COS(2.3 * theta)
    sx3(I%) = x3 * SpinCTiltC + y3 * SpinCTiltS - zSpinS
    sy3(I%) = -x3 * TiltSin + y3 * TiltCos

' Calculate the finger tip position
    x4 = x3 - 25 * SIN(3 * theta)
    y4 = y3 + 25 * COS(3 * theta)
    sx4(I%) = x4 * SpinCTiltC + y4 * SpinCTiltS - zSpinS
    sy4(I%) = -x4 * TiltSin + y4 * TiltCos

NEXT I%
END SUB
```

Finally, DrawHand is called to draw the fingers on the screen.

Subroutine
DrawHand

```
SUB DrawHand
'*********************** SUB : DrawHand ************************
'
' This routine draws the fingers on the screen
'
'*************************************************************
```

```
      COLOR col%
      WINDOW (-175, -50)-(175, 250)
      FOR I% = 0 TO 4
      LINE (sx1(I%), sy1(I%))-(sx2(I%), sy2(I%))
      LINE (sx2(I%), sy2(I%))-(sx3(I%), sy3(I%))
      LINE (sx3(I%), sy3(I%))-(sx4(I%), sy4(I%))
      CIRCLE (sx1(I%), sy1(I%)), 2, 4
      CIRCLE (sx2(I%), sy2(I%)), 1, 4
      CIRCLE (sx3(I%), sy3(I%)), 1, 4
      CIRCLE (sx4(I%), sy4(I%)), 1, 4
   NEXT I%
   END SUB
```

Transformations – spinning and tilting the model

The screen co-ordinates

The X–Y–Z reference frame can be rotated to enable the hand model to be viewed on the screen at any angle. It can be rotated about the Y-axis, called *Spin* in the program, and Z-axis, called *Tilt* in the program. These rotations are shown below in Figure 3.6 and can be represented as matrices, where S and T are the angle of Spin and Tilt respectively.

$$\text{Rotation about Y-axis, Spin} = \begin{pmatrix} \cos(S) & 0 & -\sin(S) \\ 0 & 1 & 0 \\ \sin(S) & 0 & \cos(S) \end{pmatrix}$$

$$\text{Rotation about Z-axis, Tilt} = \begin{pmatrix} \cos(T) & \sin(T) & 0 \\ -\sin(T) & \cos(T) & 0 \\ 0 & 0 & 1 \end{pmatrix}$$

So to find the screen co-ordinates: sx, sy, (sz), of a joint we must multiply the absolute co-ordinates by the above matrices, first tilting, then spinning the result.

Chapter 3

$$\begin{pmatrix} sx \\ sy \\ sz \end{pmatrix} = \begin{pmatrix} \cos(S) & 0 & -\sin(S) \\ 0 & 1 & 0 \\ \sin(S) & 0 & \cos(S) \end{pmatrix} \begin{pmatrix} \cos(T) & \sin(T) & 0 \\ -\sin(T) & \cos(T) & 0 \\ 0 & 0 & 1 \end{pmatrix} \begin{pmatrix} x \\ y \\ z \end{pmatrix}$$

This gives the rotation matrix:

$$\begin{pmatrix} sx \\ sy \\ sz \end{pmatrix} = \begin{pmatrix} \cos(S)\cos(T) & \cos(S)\sin(T) & -\sin(S) \\ -\sin(T) & \cos(T) & 0 \\ \sin(S)\cos(T) & \sin(S)\sin(T) & \cos(S) \end{pmatrix} \begin{pmatrix} x \\ y \\ z \end{pmatrix}$$

Thus if we multiply the matrix of joint positions, in terms of (x,y,z) by the rotation matrix the product is the new positions so for the middle joint of the finger, the screen co-ordinates would be:

$sx_2 = x_2.cos(S).cos(T) + y_2.cos(S).sin(T) - z_2.sin(S)$
$sy_2 = -x_2.sin(T) + y_2.cos(T)$

There is no sz_2 because the monitor screen is only 2D.

Figure 3.6
Rotations of the hand

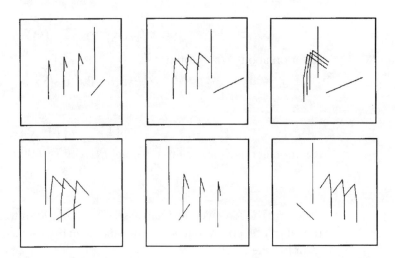

In the program the *sines* and *cosines* of the Spin and Tilt, and their products are calculated beforehand, and only recalculated when the rotation angles are changed. This means that each time the program calculates the positions for the entire hand it only has 28 trigonometric calculations. These transformations, which control the angle from which the hand is viewed, are implemented in the routine `CalcSpinTilt` shown below.

Subroutine
CalcSpinTilt

```
SUB CalcSpinTilt
' ************************ SUB: CalcSpinTilt *************************
'
' This calculates the sin and cos of Spin% and Tilt% and their products
' for use in the equations to calculate screen co-ords.
'
' *****************************************************************
    Spinrad = Spin% * pi / 180
    Tiltrad = Tilt% * pi / 180
    SpinCos = COS(Spinrad)
    SpinSin = SIN(Spinrad)
    TiltCos = COS(Tiltrad)
    TiltSin = SIN(Tiltrad)
    SpinCTiltC = SpinCos * TiltCos
    SpinCTiltS = SpinCos * TiltSin
END SUB
```

To demonstrate the power of this routine try replacing the fixed viewing angles with constantly changing values, and the hand will spin dramatically. In addition to the rotations shown above we can move and scale an image by the use of the following transformation matrices.

$$\begin{pmatrix} SX \\ SY \\ SZ \end{pmatrix} = \begin{pmatrix} scaleX & 0 & 0 & transX \\ 0 & scaleY & 0 & transY \\ 0 & 0 & scaleZ & transZ \end{pmatrix} \begin{pmatrix} x \\ y \\ z \end{pmatrix}$$

Where SX is the transformed value of X, $scaleX$ is the new size of X, and $transX$ is the displacement of X.

If we multiply these additional matrices by the rotation matrix then we form a total transformation matrix shown below:

$$\begin{pmatrix} scaleX * cos(theta), & scaleX * sin(theta) * sin(beta), & sin(theta) * cos(beta) * (-scaleX), & transX \\ 0, & scaleY * cos(beta), & scaleY * sin(beta), & transY \\ scaleZ * sin(theta) & sin(beta) * cos(theta) * (-scaleZ), & scaleZ * cos(theta) * cos(beta), & transZ \end{pmatrix}$$

Figure 3.7 shows the translation of a cube and the keyboard control characters. The program which performs this translation is called, ROTCUBE, and is shown below. The individual transformation matrices are used: this allows the program to be dissected and used for individual rotations. The combined translation matrix is used in the program PRESFACE which can be found in Chapter 4.

Program
ROTCUBE

```
    apage = 0: vpage = 1
'setup cube
    notrip = 8
    nolin = 12
DIM SHARED a(4, 4)
DIM xp(notrip), X(notrip), xx(notrip), xxx(notrip), xxxx(notrip),
xxxxx(notrip), yp(notrip), y(notrip), yy(notrip), yyy(notrip), yyyy(notrip),
yyyyy(notrip), z(notrip), zz(notrip), zzz(notrip), zzzz(notrip),
zzzzz(notrip), linfrom(nolin), linto(_nolin)

'corner points
    X(1)=50:X(2)=50:X(3)=50:X(4)=50:X(5)=-50:X(6)=-50:X(7)=-50:X(8)=-50
    y(1)=50:y(2)=50:y(3)=-50:y(4)=-50:y(5)=50:y(6)=50:y(7)=-50:y(8)=-50
    z(1)=50:z(2)=-50:z(3)=50:z(4)=-50:z(5)=50:z(6)=-50:z(7)=50:z(8)=-50
'line connection
    linfrom(1)=1:linfrom(2)=2:linfrom(3)=4:linfrom(4)=3:linfrom(5)=5
    linto(1)=2:linto(2)=4:linto(3)=3:linto(4)=1:linto(5)=6
    linfrom(6)=6:linfrom(7)=8:linfrom(8)=7:linfrom(9)=1:linfrom(10)=2
    linto(6)=8:linto(7)=7:linto(8)=5:linto(9)=5:linto(10)=6
    linfrom(11)=3:linfrom(12)=4
    linto(11)=7:linto(12)=8
    scaleX = 1
    transX = 0
    transY = 0
    transZ = 0
    theta = 0
    beta = 0
    gama = 0
    dist = 500
    ppd = 20
DO
    SCREEN 9, , apage, vpage
    CLS
    COLOR 7
    in$ = INKEY$
    IF in$ = "," THEN theta = theta -.1
    IF in$ = "/" THEN theta = theta +.1
'rotation matrix Yaxis
    a(1, 1) = COS(theta): a(1, 2) = 0: a(1, 3) = -SIN(theta): a(1, 4) = 0
    a(2, 1) = 0: a(2, 2) = 1: a(2, 3) = 0: a(2, 4) = 0
    a(3, 1) = SIN(theta): a(3, 2) = 0: a(3, 3) = COS(theta): a(3, 4) = 0
    a(4, 1) = 0: a(4, 2) = 0: a(4, 3) = 0: a(4, 4) = 1
```

```
'multiply co-ordinate matrix by translation matrix
    FOR n = 1 TO notrip
    xx(n) = (a(1, 1) * X(n)) + (a(1, 2) * y(n)) + (a(1, 3) * z(n)) + a(1, 4)
    yy(n) = (a(2, 1) * X(n)) + (a(2, 2) * y(n)) + (a(2, 3) * z(n)) + a(2, 4)
    zz(n) = (a(3, 1) * X(n)) + (a(3, 2) * y(n)) + (a(3, 3) * z(n)) + a(3, 4)
NEXT n
    IF in$ = "l" THEN beta = beta + .05
    IF in$ = "." THEN beta = beta - .05
'rotation matrix Xaxis
    a(1, 1) = 1: a(1, 2) = 0: a(1, 3) = 0: a(1, 4) = 0
    a(2, 1) = 0: a(2, 2) = COS(beta): a(2, 3) = SIN(beta): a(2, 4) = 0
    a(3, 1) = 0: a(3, 2) = -SIN(beta): a(3, 3) = COS(beta): a(3, 4) = 0
    a(4, 1) = 0: a(4, 2) = 0: a(4, 3) = 0: a(4, 4) = 1
'multiply co-ordinate matrix by translation matrix
    FOR n = 1 TO notrip
    xxx(n) = (a(1, 1) * xx(n)) + (a(1, 2) * yy(n)) + (a(1, 3) * zz(n)) + a(1, 4)
    yyy(n) = (a(2, 1) * xx(n)) + (a(2, 2) * yy(n)) + (a(2, 3) * zz(n)) + a(2, 4)
    zzz(n) = (a(3, 1) * xx(n)) + (a(3, 2) * yy(n)) + (a(3, 3) * zz(n)) + a(3, 4)
NEXT n
    IF in$ = "\" THEN transX = transX + 10
    IF in$ = "x" THEN transX = transX - 10
    IF in$ = "a" THEN transY = transY + 10
    IF in$ = "z" THEN transY = transY - 10
    IF in$ = "s" THEN scaleX = scaleX + .1
    IF in$ = "d" THEN scaleX = scaleX - .1
'translation matrix
    a(1, 1) = scaleX: a(1, 2) = 0: a(1, 3) = 0: a(1, 4) = transX
    a(2, 1) = 0: a(2, 2) = scaleX: a(2, 3) = 0: a(2, 4) = transY
    a(3, 1) = 0: a(3, 2) = 0: a(3, 3) = scaleX: a(3, 4) = transZ
    a(4, 1) = 0: a(4, 2) = 0: a(4, 3) = 0: a(4, 4) = 1
'multiply co-ordinate matrix by translation matrix
FOR n = 1 TO notrip
    xxxx(n)=(a(1, 1)*xxx(n))+(a(1, 2)*yyy(n))+(a(1, 3)*zzz(n))+a(1, 4)
    yyyy(n)=(a(2, 1)*xxx(n))+(a(2, 2)*yyy(n))+(a(2, 3)*zzz(n))+a(2, 4)
    zzzz(n)=(a(3, 1)*xxx(n))+(a(3, 2)*yyy(n))+(a(3, 3)*zzz(n))+a(3, 4)
NEXT n
    IF in$ = "k" THEN gama = gama - .1
IF in$ = ";" THEN gama = gama + .1
'rotation matrix Xaxis
    a(1, 1) = COS(gama): a(1, 2) = SIN(gama): a(1, 3) = 0: a(1, 4) = 0
    a(2, 1) = -SIN(gama): a(2, 2) = COS(gama): a(2, 3) = 0: a(2, 4) = 0
    a(3, 1) = 0: a(3, 2) = 0: a(3, 3) = 1: a(3, 4) = 0
    a(4, 1) = 0: a(4, 2) = 0: a(4, 3) = 0: a(4, 4) = 1
'multiply co-ordinate matrix by translation matrix
FOR n = 1 TO notrip
    xxxxx(n)=(a(1, 1)*xxxx(n))+(a(1, 2)*yyyy(n))+(a(1, 3)*zzzz(n))+a(1, 4)
    yyyyy(n)=(a(2, 1)*xxxx(n))+(a(2, 2)*yyyy(n))+(a(2, 3)*zzzz(n))+a(2, 4)
    zzzzz(n)=(a(3, 1)*xxxx(n))+(a(3, 2)*yyyy(n))+(a(3, 3)*zzzz(n))+a(3, 4)
    xp(n) = xxxxx(n)
    yp(n) = yyyyy(n)
NEXT n
```

Figure 3.7
Translation of
cube

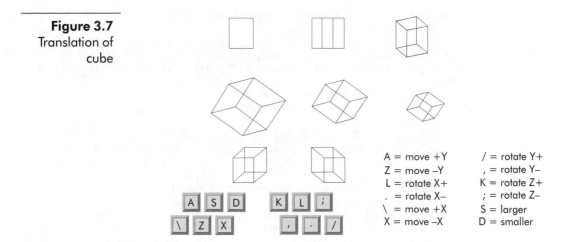

A = move +Y   / = rotate Y+
Z = move –Y   , = rotate Y–
L = rotate X+   K = rotate Z+
. = rotate X–   ; = rotate Z–
\ = move +X   S = larger
X = move –X   D = smaller

Display survey

Introduction

Most people associate virtual reality with the head-mounted display (HMD), the helmet which excludes the view of the real world and provides the most direct experience of virtual worlds. However, there are a number of other display options which are increasingly being adopted. In this section we look at head-mounted displays, and consider the alternatives.

Head-mounted displays

The simplest form of head-mounted display is a pair of display screens and some clever optics packaged together so that they may be worn on the head. The optics allow the user to focus on a display screen several inches from their face, and increase the field of view of the displayed image. Normally the lenses used are anemorphic lenses, similar to those used by the film industry to produce panoramic, cinemascope films. The *Virtuality Visette®* is one of the most widely available head-mounted devices. It has two colour LCDs, with a resolution of 276×372 pixels and a field of view adjustable to between $90°$ and $120°$ and uses aspheric optical eyepieces custom designed for the 1.3" AMTFT. Most HMD manufacturers initially used 2.7" colour LCD displays which *Sony* had developed for their 'Watchmen' TV. As they were mass produced they were available at a reasonable cost, but their resolution left a lot to be desired. They had only 24,000 elements as compared with 175,000 for some personal computer screens. The result is that the image appears pixellated (broken up into individual elements).

Figure 3.8 The Visette® head-mounted display. Reproduced by kind permission of *Virtuality Entertainment Ltd*, Leicester, UK

A number of displays, which are just starting to appear commercially, have 1280×960 pixels; however, these use cathode ray tubes which are heavier than LCD displays and have the added hazard of requiring several thousand volts to drive them. They are similar to the low resolution versions used in video viewfinders, and are used by the military in head-up displays. Once you have solved issues relating to the display technology and the optics, one big problem is packaging them safely in a form that is light enough to be worn for an extended period. Two alternatives to head-mounted displays are stereo shutter glasses and head-coupled displays, both are attempts at solving the weight problem

Stereo glasses

Designers are working towards an ideal or lightweight display which may be worn in a similar way to a pair of glasses. One approach is to use liquid-crystal shutter glasses with lenses made of a liquid crystal material which can be switched rapidly form clear to opaque and back again.

Figure 3.9
Stereo glasses

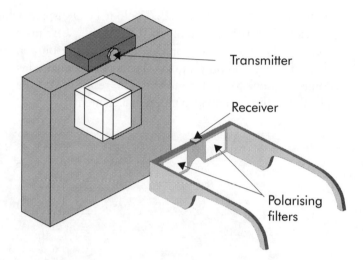

The glasses are used to view a monitor on which is displayed alternating right-eye and left-eye views of an object. The right and left views are slightly shifted, so that the brain is tricked into believing there is depth in the scene. The glasses' shutters are synchronized with the monitor display using infra-red signals, so that only left eye views are revealed to the left eye and right eye views to the right. The technique is similar to the anaglph method which uses red–green filters to present different views to each eye, and is described later in the chapter.

Head-coupled displays

Head-coupled displays are like a large pair of binoculars supported by a movable, counter-balanced arm. As the supporting arm takes the weight of the unit, the displays can be heavier and therefore offer better resolution and a wider field of view than head-mounted displays.

VR rooms large-screen projection displays

In industrial applications, head-mounted displays offer a number of disadvantages including the isolation of the participants and the high cost of providing multi-viewer systems. The combination of large-screen projection systems and shutter glasses allow a large number of uses to share the 'virtual experience' in a 'VR room', and this is the approach being taken by a number of industry uses. Examples include the 'cave' at the University of Illinois.

Chapter 4

Tracking devices

This chapter looks at tracking systems which allow the motion of a hand or head to be sensed and the information used to move objects, or change the view point, on the screen. We start with a survey of existing tracking methods, looking briefly at electromagnetic, ultrasonic, mechanical and optical techniques. Most commercial systems rely on the electromagnetic technique, measuring strengths of electromagnetic field, or the ultrasonic technique, measuring time-of-flight of ultrasound pulses. We then look at two designs which will follow hand movements in two dimensions. The first uses a mechanical approach, with potentiometers measuring the angles between rigid spars. Two spars and two potentiometers are sufficient to make a mechanical tracker which can follow a hand in one plane. Adding a third potentiometer to form a 'waist' joint would allow this tracker to follow movement in three dimensions.

The second design uses an ultrasonic transmitter and two ultrasonic receivers to track hand movement. Instead of using the time-of-flight of sound pulses, it is possible to construct a simple tracker by measuring signal level at each receiver.

A survey of tracking systems

One of the key elements in any virtual reality system is a reliable three dimensional motion-tracking device. A number of techniques are available and most require a physical sensor to be attached to the object to be tracked; this is known as *active tracking*. The alternative to active tracking is passive tracking which does not require a sensor mounted on the object, but uses cameras to optically determine position and orientation. This latter approach, although offering a tremendous increase in freedom of motion to the user, requires very complex processing and is still at the research stage.

Active tracking, although simpler, still has problems associated with the basic physics of the devices used; the biggest problem being 'tracker lag' due to the slow response time of the sensors.

Electromagnetic

This is one of the most popular methods of tracking, because of the small sensor size and freedom of movement. A low frequency signal generated by a control box sequentially excites three small coils of wire in the source to create three magnetic fields. Three small sense coils mounted at right angles to one another each detect the three fields. This gives a total of nine measurements which are then processed by the control box to produce six values for position and orientation in three-dimensional space. This technique was first developed (about ten years ago), by a company called *Polhemus* for military applications. The *Polhemus* system is now used by many other companies. It has evolved into a reliable and accurate method of tracking because it does not use line of sight, so obstruction by objects does not cause a problem. However, metal structures in the building fabrication and nearby computer monitors can generate magnetic fields capable of overwhelming or distorting the test signal. Special high speed signal conditioning filters have been introduced to reduce mistracking problems.

Figure 4.1 The Polhemus FASTRAK® system. Reproduced by permission of *Polhemus Incorporated*

Ultrasonic

This is one of the cheapest methods of tracking objects and uses ultrasonic transducers and small microphones. In some commercial systems the transducers are mounted at each corner of a triangular frame and set approximately one foot apart. A smaller triangle, the sensor, contains the microphones. This would be mounted on top of a helmet for head tracking. Figure 4.2 shows a *CrystalEyes* VR system with electronic stereo eyewear, and a head tracking system with six degrees of freedom.

Figure 4.2 CrystalEyes head tracker and stereo eyewear. Reproduced by permission of *StereoGraphics Corporation*

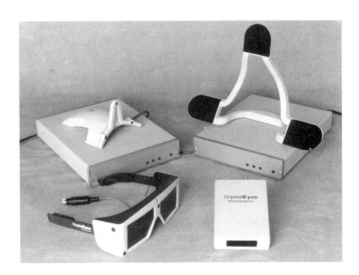

The ultrasonic transducers emit a high frequency sound pulse which is picked up by all three microphones. A signal processor either using the computer or mounted on a separate board measures the delay and therefore the distance between each transducer and each set of microphones. Next the nine distances measured are processed via triangulation to yield the detected position.

The ultrasonic system has one advantage over the electromagnetic: sound pulses are received rapidly, but the electromagnetic system takes time for a voltage to build up in the search coil. Although this kind of delay is small, possibly milliseconds, it detracts significantly from the CPU process time before triangulation and 3D graphics have even taken place, leading to poor update of the display, which is termed *lag*.

An obvious disadvantage with the ultrasonic system is that the sensors must have direct line of sight. Acoustic reflections and ambient noise can also cause problems. For instance, jangling a bunch of keys will generate harmonics in the 40KHz region which will register on the transducers. However, the low cost and ease of signal detection make ultrasonics a popular choice.

Mechanical

A mechanical system of motion tracking involves the use of a physical connection of the object to a reference point. A robotic arm or boom with a series of joints fitted with sensors that record the angular motion is generally used. The joined sensors are generally potentiometers which provide a linear change in voltage with change in joint angle. These sensors are very accurate with no processing or propagation delays in the sensor operation. This method is therefore very fast and accurate for position measurement, the main limitation being the lack of freedom of motion, see Figure 4.3.

Optical

Several techniques of optical tracking have been developed, including the use of three head-mounted cameras to view patterns of LEDs on the ceiling, and a single camera used to view a circle of LEDs mounted on a plane.

Designs for tracking systems

Tracking head and hand position and orientation swiftly and accurately is a challenging technical problem. We look first at two solutions adopted by early researchers in the area using mechanical and optical methods.

Figure 4.3
Mechanical
head-tracker

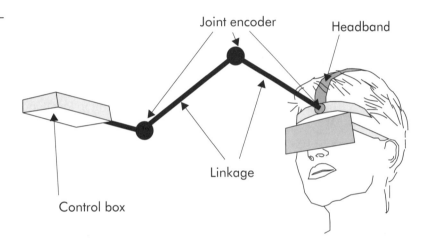

Joint encoder

Headband

Linkage

Control box

Design for a mechanical tracker

In his early work on head-mounted displays, Ivan Sutherland used a mechanical tracker, nicknamed *The Sword of Damocles*, to monitor head position.

Mechanical trackers are comparatively simple to construct and have none of the disadvantages of lag inherent in electromagnetic systems, their main problem is that they do restrict the user's movement. The design for a simple tracker, best suited to tracking hand position, is shown in Figure 4.4.

We chose a design based on the structure of a robot, with three rotational joints linked by three rigid spars. If the angle of rotation of each of the joints is measured, then the position of the end point of the arm in space may be calculated.

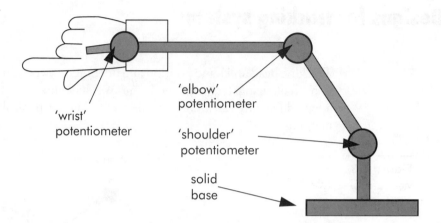

Figure 4.4
Mechanical
hand-tracker

'wrist'
potentiometer

'elbow'
potentiometer

'shoulder'
potentiometer

solid
base

In the configuration shown, the tracker will follow hand movements in 2D. To extend into 3D, a 'waist' joint must be added to allow the whole arm to rotate about the base. Addition of 2 more joints at the robot 'wrist' would also allow the orientation of the hand to be calculated.

Measuring joint angles

The joint angles are measured using potentiometers. A potentiometer consists of a resistive track connected to two outer solder tags. The middle solder tag is connected to a 'wiper' which slides along the track as the shaft is rotated and picks-off an intermediate voltage corresponding to its position.

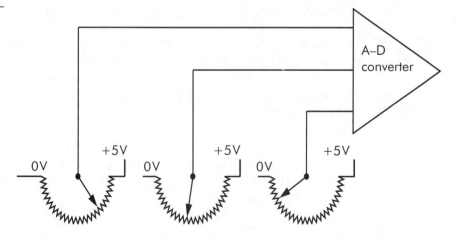

Figure 4.5
Potentiometer
interface

A–D
converter

+5V   +5V   +5V

0V   0V   0V

In our design we used three 2.2 kΩ, linear, single turn potentiometers linked together using balsa wood spars. Parts are listed in Appendix B.

Interfacing the potentiometers

The analogue voltages on the potentiometers may be read by the computer using an analogue-to-digital converter, in a similar way to the sensor voltages in Chapter 2. The same input software may be used and the circuit is the same except that the potentiometers replace the light-dependent resistors in the glove design, as shown in Figure 4.5.

Converting from joint angles to Cartesian (X, Y, Z) space

Once the voltages representing the joint angles have been read into the computer they must be converted, using trigonometry, to a value which gives the position of the joints of the arm in cartesian space.

To draw the position of the hand on the screen for a simple two-link tracker, you will first have to convert the potentiometer voltages received at the computer to angular measurements. The (X,Y) position of the end of the two-link tracker will be given by:

$$\begin{pmatrix} X \\ Y \end{pmatrix} = \begin{pmatrix} l_1 \cos(\theta_1) + l_2 \cos(\theta_1 + \theta_2) \\ l_1 \sin(\theta_1) + l_2 \sin(\theta_1 + \theta_2) \end{pmatrix}$$

where:

Figure 4.6

l_1 is the length of the first spar

l_2 is the length of the second spar

θ_1 is the angle between the first spar and the X-axis

θ_2 is the angle between the second spar and a coordinate X1 projected forwards from and parallel to the first spar

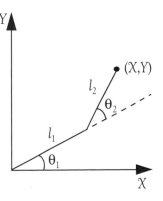

Design for an ultrasonic tracker

For those confident of their electronic skills and who seek a challenge, the development of an ultrasonic tracker is an interesting project. Most commercial ultrasonic trackers rely on timing the flight of pulses between transmitters and receivers, either using timers built in electronic hardware, or in software. The position of the transmitter can be calculated by finding the distance between each of the receivers and the transmitter by measuring the time it takes for the sound to be received by each of the sensors. Using trigonometry, the three distances may be converted to a position in (X, Y, Z) space. However, constructing a system using these principles is rather too complex for a home project; here we consider a less demanding approach.

Figure 4.7
Ultrasonic
tracker layout

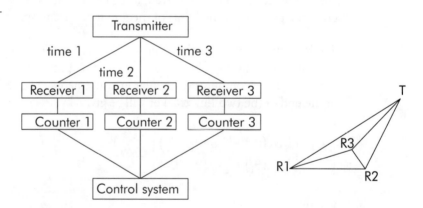

Tracking by signal strength alone

A simple tracker for one axis of movement may be built using one ultrasonic transmitter and just two receivers. Instead of timing the time-of-flight of the sound, it is possible just to measure the signal level at each receiver as the transmitter is moved in the plane at right angles to the receivers. Obviously, at the mid-point between the receivers the signal level at each should be equal.

As the transmitter moves closer or further away from a receiver the signal strength will vary with distance in an approximately linear fashion. If the receiver outputs are connected to an analogue computer input, the voltage levels measured at each receiver may be used to calculate the transmitter position along the axis.

Building the ultrasonic location sensor

This section covers how to make an ultrasonic transmitter and receiver which can be used to track your hand movements and display them on the computer screen. You can use it to control a hand in a virtual world inside the computer.

The tracker design uses ultrasonic transducers – devices for transmitting and receiving ultrasonic sound waves. They are really just like the microphones and speakers used for transmitting and picking up the sound we can hear – the difference is that ultrasound is a kind of sound so high in frequency that we cannot hear it. (Though dogs can, having a greater range of hearing than humans). The ultrasonic transmitter changes electrical pulses into ultrasonic sound waves and the receiver changes them back into electrical pulses again. You can program your computer to translate the electrical pulses from the receiver into position readings and display them on the screen.

Figure 4.8
Ultrasonic
transmitter/
receiver circuits

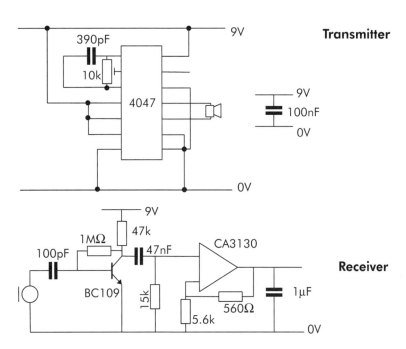

Things you will need

These are the components you will need to make the ultrasonic transmitters and reciever. You can buy them from electronic shops or send for them from electronic suppliers.

For the transmitter:

- 40 kHz Ultrasonic transducer (transmitter)
- 4047 IC
- 10k preset resistor VR
- 390 pF capacitor C1
- 100 nF capacitor C2
- 14 pin DIL IC socket
- 9 V PP3 battery
- PP3 PCB mounted battery holder
- 12 cm × 3 cm piece of strip board with 12 strips of copper

For the receiver:

- 40 kHz ultrasonic transducer (receiver)
- BC 109 transistor T1
- CA3130 op-amp IC
- 100 pF capacitor C1, 47 nF capacitor C2
- 1 μF electrolytic capacitor C3
- 22 nF capacitor C4
- 1 M 1/4 W resistor R1
- 47 k 1/4 W resistor R2
- 15 k 1/4 W resistor R3
- 560 Ω 1/4 resistor R4
- 5.6 k 1/4 W resistor R5
- 25 pin D-Type connector
- 8 pin DIL IC socket
- 10 cm × 7 cm piece of strip board with 29 copper strips
- 9 V PP3 battery
- PP3 PCB mounted battery holder

For both transmitter and receiver you will need:

- solder
- electrical soldering iron
- insulated copper wire
- wire cutters

- ▸ wire strippers
- ▸ copper-track cutting tool

Making the receiver

In Figure 4.9 you can see the layout of the strip board and where to solder the components. You need to solder the wire and components to the back of the board where the copper track is. It is best to make the breaks in the copper strip first with the cutting tool. Then solder the IC socket in first. The battery holder, wires, resistor and capacitors should be soldered next, then the transistor last. When all the soldering is finished the IC can be plugged into the socket. Take care to ensure that all the legs of the IC go into the correct holes of the sockets.

Figure 4.9
Receiver strip
board layout

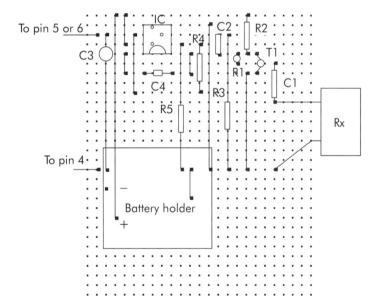

Making the transmitter

The transmitter should be built in the same way as the receiver. In the picture below you can see the layout of the strip board and where to solder the components. Once built, the circuit will need to be 'tuned'. The best way to do this is to connect the receivers to a computer.

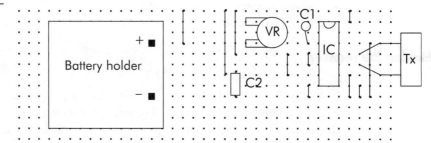

Figure 4.10
Transmitter strip
board layout

Connecting to a computer

The receiver can be connected to a computer using the D-type connector and an A–D card, such as the *Roldec* card. Connect one receiver to pin 5 of the D-type connector, and the other receiver to pin 6. Both ground lines can be connected together, and on to pin 4. If you then load the program ULTRACK from the demo disk, you will see the signal being received displayed as a circle on the screen.

To tune the transmitter, hold it next to the receiver and adjust the preset resistor until the display on the computer moves. Then position the two receivers 1 m apart, pointing in the same direction, and move the transmitter backwards and forwards along an axis approximately 0.5 m in front of the receivers. The circle on the screen should move left and right in response to your movement of the transmitter.

Tracker applications

Virtual sculpture

One of the most spectacular applications of tracker technology is shown in Figure 4.11. Catherine Ikam, a French sculptress, used an ultrasonic/infra-red tracker, held by the viewer, to control the movement and expressions of a gigantic face back-projected onto a 10 m high screen. A visitor enters a darkened room and is confronted by a large blue face floating in space. On approaching the mask-like head, it inclines forward as if acknowledging the newcomer to its domain. Moving to the right or left and L'Autre ('The Other') swings round to follow.

Whatever the visitor does is registered in some way: the face winks, nods, smiles and mutters silently, apparently omniscient. The effect of being leered at, smiled at, and seemingly pursued, by a 10m high glowing blue face in a darkened room is quite eerie.

Figure 4.11
Virtual sculpture
Reproduced by
permission of
Catherine Ikam

The program ROTCUBE can be adapted to produce our own virtual sculpture in conjunction with the ultrasonic tracker. The points and lines of the cube are redefined to produce an angular face. A mouse on the bottom of the screen represents the detected position of the observer as they move from left to right so the face follows them around the room. The program is called PERSFACE and is listed below. Figure 4.12 shows screen dumps of the program in action.

Program
PERSFACE

```
apage = 0: vpage = 1
'setup face
    notrip = 18
    nolin = 18
DIM SHARED a(4, 4)
DIM xp(notrip), x(notrip), xx(notrip), xxx(notrip), xxxx(notrip), yp(notrip),
y(notrip), yy(notrip), yyy(notrip), yyyy(notrip), z(notrip), zz(notrip), zzz(notrip),
zzzz(notrip), linfrom(nolin), linto(nolin)
'corner points
'line connection
    linto(11)= 9: linto(12)= 10: linto(13)= 3: linto(14)= 3: linto(15)= 13
    linfrom(16)= 12: linfrom(17)= 14: linfrom(3)= 16: linfrom(18)= 1
    linto(16)= 13: linto(17)= 15: linto(3)= 17: linto(18)= 18
    transX= 0: scaleX= 2
    transY= 0: scaleY= 2
    transZ= 0: scaleZ= 2
    theta= 0
    beta= 0
    gama= 0
    dist= -500
    ppd= 20
DO
    SCREEN 9, , apage, vpage
    CLS
    COLOR 7
    in$ = INKEY$
CALL readtracker
IF in$= "," THEN theta= theta  .1: beta= beta    (.01*SGN(theta)):transX= transX + 10
IF in$= "/" THEN theta= theta +.1: beta= beta + (.01*SGN(theta)):transX= transX   10
'combined Y.X.T.S matrix
    a(1,1)= scaleX*COS(theta): a(1,2)= scaleX*SIN(theta)*SIN(beta)
    a(1,3)= SIN(theta)*COS(beta)*scaleX: a(1,4)= transX
    a(2,1)= 0: a(2,2)= scaleY*COS(beta): a(2,3)= scaleY*SIN(beta): a(2,4)= transY
    a(3,1)= scaleZ*SIN(theta): a(3,2)= SIN(beta)*COS(theta)*scaleZ
    a(3,3)= scaleZ*COS(theta)*COS(beta): a(3,4)= transZ
    a(4,1)= 0: a(4,2)= 0: a(4,3)= 0: a(4,4)= 1
'multiply coordinate matrix by translation matrix
FOR n = 1 TO notrip
    xx(n)= (a(1, 1)*x(n)) + (a(1, 2)*y(n)) + (a(1, 3)*z(n)) + a(1, 4)
    yy(n)= (a(2, 1)*x(n)) + (a(2, 2)*y(n)) + (a(2, 3)*z(n)) + a(2, 4)
    zz(n)= (a(3, 1)*x(n)) + (a(3, 2)*y(n)) + (a(3, 3)*z(n)) + a(3, 4)
    dd= zz(n) + dist
    xp(n)= xx(n)*(dist / dd)
    yp(n)= yy(n)*(dist / dd)
NEXT n
COLOR 7
FOR n = 1 TO nolin
LINE (xp(linfrom(n))+320, yp(linfrom(n))+170)-(xp(linto(n))+320, yp(linto(n))+170)
NEXT n
IF in$ = "l" THEN beta= beta + .02: tranY= tranY + 5
IF in$ = "." THEN beta= beta - .02: tranY= tranY - 5
d= 240 + (tranY*5): c= 200 + (transX*5)
LINE (100 + c, 100 + d)-(150 + c, 100 + d):LINE (150 + c, 100 + d)-(115 + c, 85 + d)
LINE (115 + c, 85 + d)-(100 + c, 100 + d)
SWAP apage, vpage
LOOP
```

Using virtual reality to interface with a Nanomanipulator

(Courtesy of the Department of Computer Science at the University of North Carolina at Chapel Hill and The Department of Chemistry at the University of California at Los Angeles.)

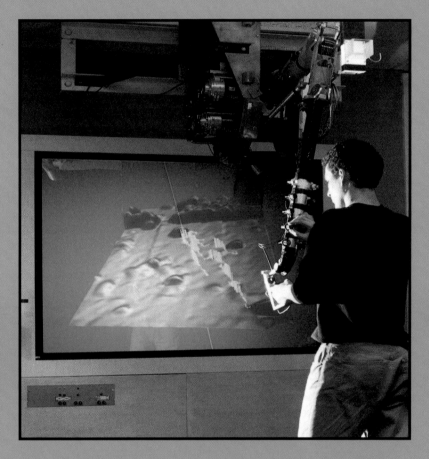

UNC Physics graduate student Mike Falvo uses the UNC/UCLA Nanomanipulator system to manoeuver a colloidal particle into a gap that has been etched into a thin gold wire. This system couples an atomic force microscope (AFM) located in the physics department with a virtual-reality interface in the computer science department to provide a telepresence system that operates over a scale difference of about 10^6. Mike directly controls the lateral position of the AFM tip; real-time force feedback, indicating surface height, allows him to guide the motion of the particle **during** manipulation, when the tip cannot scan the surface. The area under study is about 1 micron on a side. The colloidal gold particle is about 15nm across. The vertical scale has been exaggerated by a factor of five over the horizontal to bring out surface features. Yellow lines mark the progress of the tip during modification.

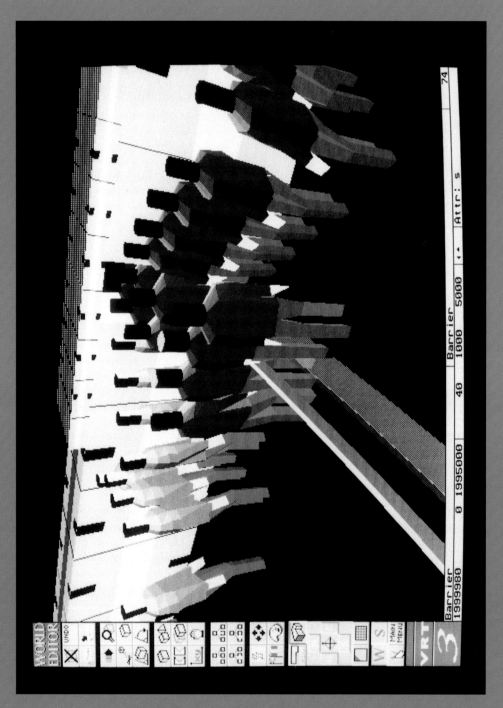

Virtual reality simulation of an evacuation
(Courtesy of Colt Virtual Reality Limited.)

Colt VR's VEGAS software showing an emergency evacuation.

Figure 4.12
DIY virtual
sculpture

 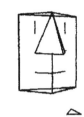 

Chapter 5

Into 3D

This chapter looks at ways of creating the illusion of 3D on the screen, which will allow the tracker developed in the last chapter to manipulate objects in a virtual 3D space.

We start by looking at the cues which the brain uses to determine the relative position and distance of objects such as: size, where the scale of a familiar object is used to determine its distance; texture, gradient and shading, where objects more distant appear darker and less refined; occlusion, where a closer object covers or obscures a more distant one; and various forms of perspective, linear and aerial. These monocular depth cues can produce a powerful impression of three dimensionality. A simple cube is used to demonstrate the use of the perspective transformation and hidden-line removal. Later in the chapter the principles of solid modelling are explored where we consider problems of polygon filling, and hidden-surface removal. Stereoscopic transformations are demonstrated through the use of algorithms and program examples, which allow each eye to receive a separate image, producing the strongest illusion of three dimensional space.

Depth cues for spatial vision

The brain uses visual 'cues' to determine the size and location of objects in 3D space. One basic cue is that an object that appears smaller will be judged farther away than one appearing bigger. The brain uses three basic types of depth and perception cues: monocular cues, physiological cues and stereoscopic cues.

Monocular depth cues

Monocular depth cues only rely on information from one eye: either static or in motion. The static cues are shading, size, texture gradient, linear perspective, aerial perspective and occlusion; examples of these are shown in Figure 5.1.

Figure 5.1
Monocular
depth cues

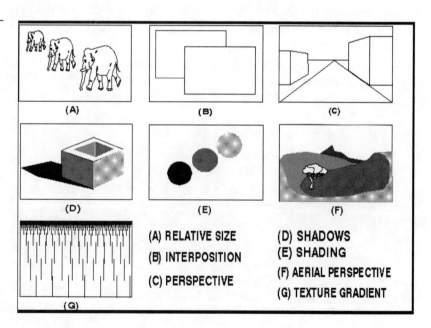

(A) RELATIVE SIZE   (D) SHADOWS
(B) INTERPOSITION   (E) SHADING
(C) PERSPECTIVE   (F) AERIAL PERSPECTIVE
                     (G) TEXTURE GRADIENT

The following explore these briefly.

Size   An object that appears smaller will be judged farther away than one appearing bigger.

Occlusion   If an object is partially obscured by another, it will appear
           to be further away.

Shading   The variation in intensity of light or colour across an
           object provide powerful depth cues, as do the shadows
           cast by an object.

The effectiveness of the cues will vary with the circumstances. Some
observers rate hiding (or *occlusion*), as the most effective, followed by
the kinetic depth effect (or *motion parallax*), and then stereopsis. Motion
parallax relies on relative motion between viewpoint and object being
different at different depths in a scene. It is a very powerful cue, particularly if the viewpoint is rocked, rather than rotated. Stereopsis, the
perception of depth through combining two slightly different views of
one scene, is a particularly powerful cue when there are few perspective
lines. It forms the basis of stereo display technology such as head-
mounted displays and stereo flicker glasses.

Perspective: Changes in the appearance of an object as it recedes into
the distance are known as perspective.

Aerial perspective: The change in brightness and colour saturation
with distance is one form of perspective. Due to moisture and dust in the
atmosphere, light from far off objects becomes duller than light from
closer objects.

Linear perspective: The further you are away from an object, the
smaller the image projected onto the retina. Thus, when we look at a
building we see that the lines formed by the roof and ground appear to
converge.

Texture gradient: Textures of objects look coarse and well defined
when close, and finer when further away.

All of the monocular vision cues have been used by artists for centuries
and are also used to create the illusion of depth in virtual environments.
Perhaps the best known, and one of the most effective, is the checker-
board floor, shown in Figure 5.2, which relies on linear perspective to
give a feeling of depth.

Figure 5.2
Chequer board
in perspective

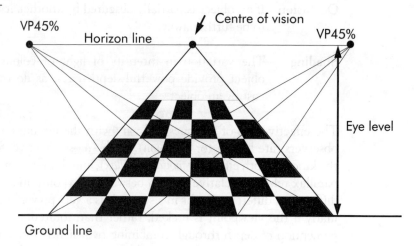

Figure 5.2
Chequer board
in perspective

Creating a perspective grid

We will use the chequer board of Figure 5.2 to demonstrate perspective laws which are implemented in the software demonstration PGRID.

If we take the sides of the board and extend them into the background they meet at a central point called the *centre of vision* (CV). Extending the front edge of the board to the left and right of forms the *ground line* (GL), a line parallel to this but placed at the CV forms the *horizon line* (HL). The perpendicular distance between these lines is called the *eye level* (EL) which is the height above the ground from which the scene is viewed.

If we now take the diagonal lines and extend them to the horizon line they meet at two points called the *vanishing points* (VP). Joining the points where these diagonal lines cross the horizontal lines, which end at the CV, with lines parallel to the ground line forms the receding scale. Thus if we know the size of the board, the number of squares and the viewing height, we can construct a perspective view.

Figure 5.3
Changing the
viewing height

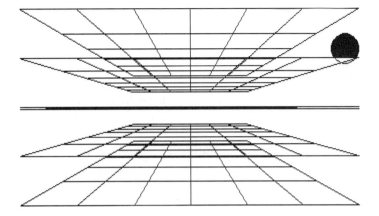

The construction of the perspective grid is divided into two parts: the drawing of the horizontal lines and the drawing of the vertical lines.

Horizontal lines

As the horizontal lines recede into the background they move backwards and shorten.

Variables	Description
EyeHgt	Eye Level
SizeSqr	Dimensions of square
NoSqr	Number of squares
OX, OY	Origin of grid
Height	Height of line
Length	Length of line
LineNo	Line Number
DigLen	Diagonal length

The height and length of the horizontal lines can be determined by calculating the position where the diagonal lines, which end at the VP, cross the horizontal lines, which end at the CV, as shown below.

```
theta= ATN((SizeSqr*(NoSqr - 1)) / EyeHgt)
altha= ATN((SizeSqr*LineNo) / EyeHgt)
gama= (3.14 - altha - theta)
DigLen= (EyeHgt*SIN(altha)) / SIN(gama)
```

```
Length= DigLen * SIN(theta)
Height= (DigLen * COS(theta)) - EyeHgt
LINE(OX, OY-Height)-(OX-Length+(SizeSqr*((NoSqr+2)/2)), OY-Height)
```

Vertical lines

As the vertical lines move away from the centre of the grid the spacing between the lines decreases as they approach the CV.

Variables	Description
HLsize	Horizon line square
GLsize	Ground line square

The length of the vertical line has already been determined by the last horizontal line, the line spacing at ground level is determined from the square size and the number of squares. The line spacing at the horizon line end of the grid is calculated by dividing the final horizontal line length by the number of squares.

```
HLsize= (Length - (SizeSqr*((NoSqr + 2) / 2))) / (NoSqr - 1)
GLsize= (SizeSqr*LineNo)
LINE(OX - (HLsize*(LineNo - 1)), OY - Height) - (OX + GLsize, OY + EyeHgt)
```

Figure 5.3 shows the effect of altering the viewing height within the PGRID program. If we use the spinning-cube program ROTCUBE, (see Chapter 3), the co-ordinates are in terms of X, Y, Z. We can introduce perspective into the Z-plane by specifying the distance of the horizon line from the centre, or axis of rotation, of the cube as shown in Figure 5.4.

Figure 5.4
Calculating
perspective

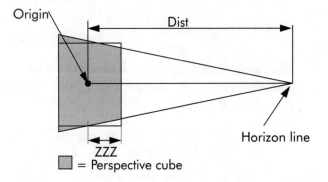

The effect of perspective is achieved by differentially scaling those points in front and behind the origin of the cube. This scale is determined through the equation below where:

```
dist= distance from the origin of the object to the horizon
ZZZ= the Z coordinate of a point on the cube relative to the origin.
X= X * dist/(ZZZ + dist)
Y= Y * dist/(ZZZ + dist)
```

The effects of this perspective transform are shown in Figure 5.5 and in the software demonstration CUBE.

Figure 5.5
Cube with and
without
perspective

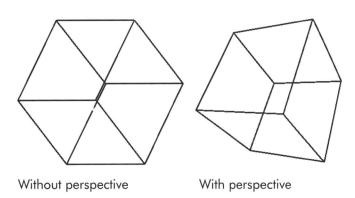

Without perspective   With perspective

Motion parallax

Moving your head from side-to-side appears to make close objects move faster than those further away. This is because closer objects throw larger images on the retina, which move across the retina faster than those from distance objects. Motion parallax can be created when objects themselves move, for example, a turning sign, or as here, a rotating hand model.

To run the rotating hand program, copy the contents of the subdirectory DATAGLOV onto your hard disk in C:\DATAGLOV. Enter the directory and type VR-NOGLOV. From the main menu select F for File, then O for Open, then type in the filename American. This will load a file of hand poses. Selecting V for View then D for Demo will call a demonstration of spinning hand poses. See how the spinning enhances the appearance of depth.(To exit, type F, then Q.)

Figure 5.6
Motion parallax

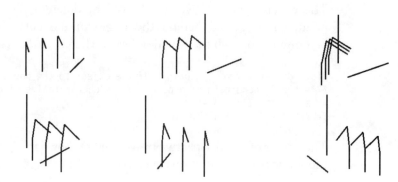

Stereoscopic cues

We can obtain depth information by comparing the views from left and right eyes. Each eye views the same scene, but they have slightly different views, and each views from a different viewing angle. This is called *binocular disparity*, or *stereopsis*. It is this cue that is used by much of the head mounted display technology to create the illusion of depth.

Anaglyphs

One of the simplest methods of implementing a stereo effect on a computer is to use anaglyphs. The anaglyphic technique, first demonstrated in 1858, creates a 3D effect using red and green filters. The 'right-hand' part of the image is projected through a green filter and the left-hand' through a red one. A green filter is placed over the left eye, and a red filter over the right eye. The green lens cancels out the green image, and the red lens the red image, with the result that each eye gets its own image. The brain combines the two to create the effect of depth. This technique was used in early Hollywood 3D movies.

3D routine

This program shows how the effect can be used with a computer to enhance the illusion of depth. It draws two images of the hand, in two different colours. Each image is rotated by 2.5° in relation to the other; in addition, the two images are separated by an offset dependent on the distance of the object from the viewer and the viewers pupil separation, to simulate the angle of view between the eyes. A stereoscopic 3D effect is seen when the image is viewed through coloured filters. A template and some instructions for making 3D glasses are given in Appendix B.

To run the 3D hand program, enter the DATAGLOV directory and type VR-NOGLOV. From the main menu, select VIEW by pressing V, then select Three-D.

In order to see the 3D image, it has to be smooth. This involved using the smooth animation technique of *double buffering*. The image is drawn on a virtual video screen, and the actual screen is only updated when the drawing is finished. This eliminates the flicker, but slows down the program. An open version of the dataglove program is included on the distribution disk for those who wish to explore or modify the program. The following software example is provided as an algorithm for the production of a stereo image.

Subroutine
ThreeD

```
SUB ThreeD
CLS
DO
    SCREEN 9, , vpage%, apage%
    CLS 1
' draws view for LEFT eye
    ANG%(0)= INT(RND*90): ANG%(1)= INT(RND*90): ANG%(2)= INT(RND*90)
    ANG%(3)= INT(RND*90): ANG%(4)= INT(RND*90)
    col%= Lcol%: Spin%= Spin% - 5
'Draw3D1
COLOR col%
WINDOW (-3000, -250)-(300, 250)
FOR I%= 0 TO 4
    PSET (0, 0)
    LINE -(sx1(I%), sy1(I%)), , , &HCCCC
    LINE(sc2(I%), sy2(I%))-(sx3(I%), sy3(I%)), , , &HCCCC
    LINE (sc3(I%), sy3(I%))-(sx4(I%), sy4(I%)), , , &HCCCC
NEXT I%
' draws view for RIGHT eye
col%= Rcol%: Spin%= Spin% + 5
'Draw3D2
COLOR col%
WINDOW (-300, -250)-(300, 250)
FOR I%= 0 TO 4
    PSET (0, 0)
    LINE -(sx1(I%), sy1(I%)), , , &H3333
    LINE (sc1(I%), sy1(I%))-(sx2(I%), sy2(I%)), , , &H3333
```

```
      LINE (sc3(I%), sy3(I%))-(sx4(I%), sy4(I%)), , , &H3333
NEXT I%
      SWAP apage%, vpage%
      key$= INKEY$
LOOP WHILE key$= ""
END SUB
```

If you wish to run the stereo hand example then copy the contents of the subdirectory DATAGLOV onto your hard disk in C:DATAGLOV. Enter the directory and type VR-NOGLV, from the main menu of the program select VIEW by pressing V then select THREE-D, the demonstration should now run. To exit the program type F then Q to exit.

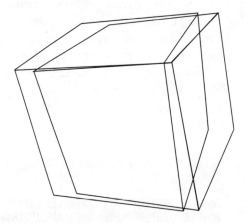

Figure 5.7
Stereoscopic cube

We can use the same technique to produce a stereoscopic cube using two stereoscopic transformation matrices, one for each eye, applied to the object before the translation matrix, as in the ROTCUBE example of Chapter 3. The results of this transformation can be seen in Figure 5.7 and in the software demonstration CUBE.

$$\begin{pmatrix} 1 & 0 & 0 & 0 \\ 0 & 1 & 0 & 0 \\ 0 & 0 & 0 & \dfrac{-1}{D_e} \\ E & 0 & 0 & 1 \end{pmatrix} \qquad \begin{pmatrix} 1 & 0 & 0 & 0 \\ 0 & 1 & 0 & 0 \\ 0 & 0 & 0 & \dfrac{-1}{D_e} \\ -E & 0 & 0 & 1 \end{pmatrix}$$

Left eye transformation   Right eye transformation

Where 'E' is half the pupil separation distance, (average distance between pupils is 62 mm), 'D_e' is the distance of the image plane.

Occlusion

A further example of depth cueing may be seen in this solid-body routine which draws a rendered image of the hand. To see the demonstration, follow the same procedure as for the THREE-D demonstration, but after pressing V for the View option, select Solid from the menu. The cue used here is occlusion, with fingers that are 'in front' obscuring the view of neighbouring fingers.

Subroutine
DrawSolidF

```
'************************ SUB: DrawSolidF *************************
'
' This routine draws solid fingers on the screen
'
'****************************************************************
WINDOW (-300, -250)-(300, 250)
FOR I%= 4 TO 0 STEP -1
        dxa= sx1(I%) - sx2(I%)
        dya= sy1(I%) - sy2(I%)
        dxya= (dxa ^ 2 + dya ^ 2) ^ .5
        x1a= sx1(I%) - 15*dya /dxya
        y1a= sy1(I%) + 15*dxa / dxya
        x2a= sx2(I%) - 15*dya / dxya
        y2a= sy2(I%) + 15*dxa / dxya
        dxb= sx2(I%) - sx3(I%)
IF dxb= 0 THEN dxb= .001
        dyb= sy2(I%) - sy3(I%)
        IF dyb= 0 THEN dyb= .0001
        dxyb= (dxb ^ 2 + dyb ^ 2) ^ .5
        x2b= sx2(I%) - 15*dyb / dxyb
        y2b= sy2(I%) + 15*dxb / dxyb
        x3b= sx3(I%) - 15*dyb / dxyb
        y3b= sy2(I%) + 15*dxy / dxyb
        dxc= sx3(I%) - sx4(I%)
IF dxc= 0 THEN dxc= .001
        dyc= sy3(I%) - sy4(I%)
IF dyc= 0 THEN dyc= .001
        dxyc= (dxc ^ 2 + dyc ^ 2) ^ .5
        x3c= sx3(I%) - 15*dyc / dxyc
        y3c= sy3(I%) + 15*dxc / dxyc
        x4c= sx4(I%) - 15*dyc / dxyc
        y4c= dy4(I%) + 15*dxy / dxyc
        col%= I% + 9
        LINE (sc1(I%), sy1(I%))-(sx2(I&+%), sy2(I%)), col%
        LINE (sx2(I%), sy2(I%))-(sx3(I%), sy3(I%)), col%
        LINE (sx3(I%), sy3(I%))-(sx4(I%), sy4(I%)), col%
```

```
CIRCLE (x4c + (sx4(I%) - x4c) / 2, y4c + (sy4(I%) - y4c) / 2), 7.5, col%
LINE (sx1(I%), sy1(I%))-(x1a, y1a), col%
LINE (x1a, y1a)-(x2a, y2a), col%
LINE (x2a, y2a)-(x2b, y2b), col%
LINE (x2b, y2b)-(x3b, y3b), col%
LINE (x3b, y3b)-(x3c, y3c), col%
LINE (x3c, y3c)-(x4c, y4c), col%
PAINT (x4c+(sx4(I%)-4xc) / 2, y4c+(sy4(I%)-y4c) / 2), col%-8, col
PAINT ((sx1(I%)+x1a+sx2(I%)) / 3, (sy1(I%)+y1a+sy2(I%)) / 3), col%
NEXT I%
END SUB
```

This shows 'thick' fingers. To do this, six more points must be calculated per finger, two for every finger segment, to determine the boundaries of the 'fill' routine. One such segment is shown in Figure 5.8.

Figure 5.8
Calculations for
solid body

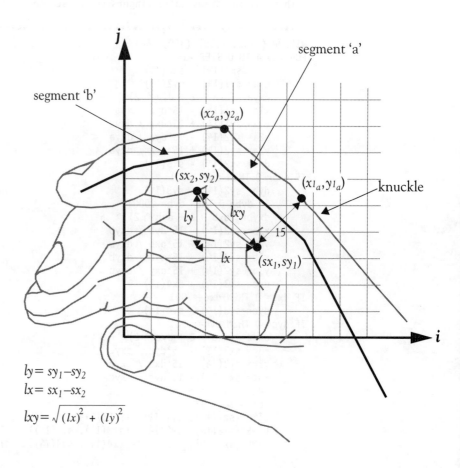

$$ly = sy_1 - sy_2$$
$$lx = sx_1 - sx_2$$
$$lxy = \sqrt{(lx)^2 + (ly)^2}$$

The unit vector from the existing point (sx_1, sy_1) to the needed point (x_{l_a}, y_{l_a}) is given by:

$$\frac{lx}{lxy}i \quad + \quad \frac{ly}{lxy}j$$

Therefore, the position of the point (x_{l_a}, y_{l_a}) is given by:

$$x_{l_a} = sx_1 - 15\,lx/lxy$$
$$y_{l_a} = sy_1 + 15\,lx/lxy$$

Once all six points are known, the outline of the finger can be drawn and filled. This gives depth cueing by occlusion: fingers closer to you cover, or occlude, portions of those behind them.

Figure 5.9
Screenshot
showing
occlusion effects

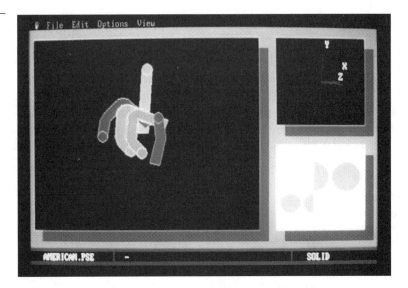

Solid modelling

As mentioned earlier, the effect of occlusion greatly enhances the realism of the virtual image by removing the false effect of transparency which occurs in wireframe models. Wireframe modelling can produce effects where the viewer does not know which lines are closest and which are more distant, thus the brain tends to switch the image. One minute a cube appears to be turning towards you the next it is turning away. This ambiguity of the image can, to some extent, be countered through the stereoscopic and perspective methods described earlier or by shading or dashing the lines which lie behind the object as shown in Figure 5.10.

Figure 5.10
Shading or
dashing of
hidden lines

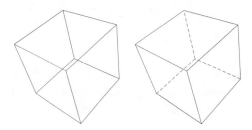

Hidden line removal

One method of producing an apparently solid object is to remove those lines which are behind the front face, or faces, of the object. In order to remove these lines we need to represent the cube in terms of faces, or facets, rather than as simply lines. A face is defined by its boundary, or edges, in the case of the cube a face is defined as the area within four edges forming a polygon. The set up data for a simple cube is shown in the program example below.

Defining facets
program
example

```
'setup cube
    notrip = 8 :'No. Corners
    nolin = 12 :'No. Lines
    nolinf = 4 :'No. Lines Per Facet
    noface = 6 :'No. Faces
    Dim Shared A(4, 4)
    Dim X(notrip), Y(notrip), Z(notrip), linfrom(nolin), linto(nolin)
    Dim linface(nolinf, noface), lineshow$(nolin)
'corner points
    X(1)=50:X(2)=50:X(3)=50:X(4)=50:X(5)=-50:X(6)=-50:X(7)=-50:X(8)=-50
    Y(1)=50:Y(2)=50:Y(3)=-50:Y(4)=-50:Y(5)=50:Y(6)=50:Y(7)=-50:Y(8)=-50
    Z(1)=50:Z(2)=-50:Z(3)=50:Z(4)=-50:Z(5)=50:Z(6)=-50:Z(7)=50:Z(8)=-50
'line connection
    linfrom(1)= 1: linfrom(2)= 2:  linfrom(3)= 4: linfrom(4)= 3: linfrom(5)= 5
    linto(1)= 2: linto(2)= 4: linto(3)= 3: linto(4)= 1: linto(5)= 6
    linfrom(6)= 6: linfrom(7)= 8: linfrom(8)= 7: linfrom(9)= 1: linfrom(10)= 2
```

```
    linto(6)= 8: linto(7)= 7: linto(8)= 5: linto(9)= 5: linto(10)= 6
    linfrom(11)= 3: linfrom(12)= 4
    linto(11)= 7: linto(12)= 8
'Define Face Edges
'Face 1
    linface(1,1)= 9:linface(2,1)= 4:linface(3,1)= 11:linface(4,1)= 8:
'Face 2
    linface(1,2)= 5:linface(2,2)= 6:linface(3,2)= 7:linface(4,2)= 8
'Face 3
    linface(1,3)= 10:linface(2,3)= 2:linface(3,3)= 12:linface(4,3)= 6
'Face 4
    linface(1,4)=1:linface(2,4)=2:linface(3,4)=3:linface(4,4)=4
'Face 5
    linface(1,5)=10:linface(2,5)=1:linface(3,5)=9:linface(4,5)=5
'Face 6
    linface(1,6)= 12:linface(2,6)=3:linface(3,6)=11:linface(4,6)=7
```

Having defined the facets of the cube we need to compare every face with every other face to determine which if any faces are between the observer and the object face as shown in Figure 5.11.

Figure 5.11
Hidden face
removal

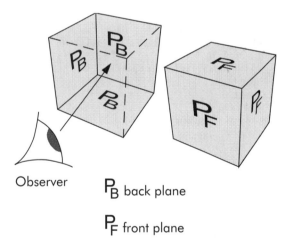

Observer

P_B back plane

P_F front plane

By calculating the equation of each plane it is possible to compare them to determine which is foremost. By only drawing the lines of the foremost face we thus eliminate the face behind. This approach only works for the simple case of a cube where partial faces are never visible. The following program example shows the calculations required to determine which faces should be drawn to remove the hidden lines.

Relative face position program example

```
Do
Screen 9, , apage, vpage
Cls
For n = 1 To nolin
    lineshow$(n) = "n"
Next n
'multiply coordinate matrix by translation matrix
'select 3 points on face to form equation of plane
For n= 1 To noface
    IV1= linfrom(linface(1, n))
    IV2= linto(linface(1, n))
    IV3= linfrom(linface(2, n))
If IV3= IV1 Or IV3= IV2 Then IV3= linto(linface(2, n))
'calculate plane ax + by + cz= d
    DX1= x(IV1) - x(IV2)
    DY1= y(IV1) - y(IV2)
    DZ1= z(IV1) - z(IV2)
    DX3= x(IV3) - x(IV2)
    DY3= y(IV3) - y(IV2)
    DZ3= z(IV3) - z(IV2)
    A= DY1*DZ3 - DY3*DZ1
    B= DZ1*DX3 - DZ3*DX1
    C= DX1*DY3 - DX3*DY1
    D= A*x(IV1) + B*y(IV1) + C*z(IV1)
    F= 1 + C*dist / D
If F > 0 Then Goto 23
'make line show equal yes for all line in this face
For nn= 1 To 4
    lineshow$(linface(nn, n))= "y"
    Next nn
23 Next n
'Draw Cube
For n= 1 To nolin
        If lineshow$(n)= "y" Then Line (xp(linfrom(n)) + 320, yp(linfrom(n))
        + 170)-(xp(linto(n)) + 320, yp(linto(n)) + 170)
Next n
    Swap apage, vpage
Loop
```

As mentioned earlier, this simple approach does not cope with the situation when a back face or line is only partially obscured; there are methods of determining which parts of lines should, or should not, be shown but they do increase the processing requirement. If the reader is interested in exploring these techniques further then we would refer you to a text on computer graphics such as *Programming Principles in Computer Graphics* by L Ammeraal, published by Wiley & Sons.

Filling facets

Having determined which facets should be drawn the next stage is to fill the facets with an appropriate colour or shade. In order to fill a facet or polygon we need to determine which pixels are within the polygon. The traditional paint routines will colour a shape by painting pixels from a point defined within the shape out until a pixel colour change is detected, which usually occurs at a boundary. If several shapes are drawn and filled then a pixel colour change may occur before the true boundary is reached – as shown in Figure 5.12.

Figure 5.12
Screen-based
fill routine

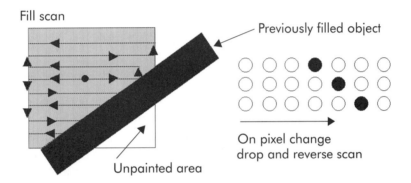

We have to use the equations of the lines which make up the edges of the face rather than screen memory to determine the boundaries of the area to be filled. The technique employed is to determine the two points, on the horizontal or vertical axis, where this axis crosses the line boundaries, and then draw a line of the fill colour between them. The axis is then indexed up or down and the next boundary points on the axis are determined and the next line is drawn. This process is repeated until the facet is filled. The value of these boundary points can be found by inputting the X or Y co-ordinate of the horizontal or vertical line into the equation of the line which represents the facet's edges.

The equation of the lines are unbounded, in that they exceed the length of the edge which is drawn and carry on to infinity either side. Unfortunately with unbounded lines every equation which represents an edge line will have a solution along a horizontal or vertical axis, as shown in Figure 5.13. Thus if we input a value of Y into the four equations which define the face we get four values of X on that line. The next stage is to determine which of these points is a true boundary so that the fill line can then be drawn between them. We can see by inspection that the true boundary points are those closest to the centre of the face.

Figure 5.13
Determination
of boundary
points

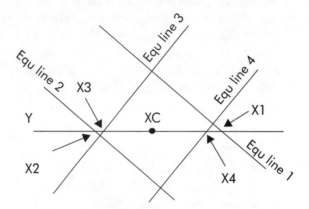

If we knew the value of the centre of the face on that particular horizontal line, (line Y in Figure 5.13), then comparing its distance from each point and selecting the smallest negative and positive values we would have determined the boundary points. This algorithm is used in the fill routine shown in the following program example.

Polygon fill paint program example

```
'fill routine
'scan up
'find centre
Ycen = Yp(centface(n)) :'Defined in set up face
ymax = -10000# :'Set Ymax very low
ymin = 10000# :'Set Ymin very high
'Find highest Y value of all face corners
For k = 1 To 4
If Yp(linfrom(linface(k,n)))> ymax Then ymax = Yp(linfrom(linface(k,n))): xymax = Xp(linfrom(linface(k, n)))
If Yp(linto(linface(k, n))) > ymax Then ymax = Yp(linto(linface(k, n))): xymax = Xp(linto(linface(k, n)))
Next k
'Find lowest value of all face corners
For k = 1 To 4
If Yp(linfrom(linface(k,n))) < ymin Then ymin=Yp(linfrom(linface(k, n))):xymin= Xp(linfrom(linface(k,n)))
If Yp(linto(linface(k, n))) < ymin Then ymin=Yp(linto(linface(k, n))):xymin=Xp(linto(linface(k, n)))
Next k
For dd = 1 To 2
    xcen = Xp(centface(n)) :'Defined in set up facet
    If dd = 2 Then yto = ymax: stp = 15: xyminmax = xymax
    If dd = 1 Then yto = ymin: stp = -15: xyminmax = xymin
For Yscan = Ycen To yto Step stp
        'check intersection
        deltaX = 0
        deltaY = 0
```

```
            'Calculate equation of lines for face
                For k = 1 To 4
                'Calculate the gradient of the line
                        Linf = linface(k, n)
                        deltaX = (Xp(linto(Linf)) - Xp(linfrom(Linf)))
                        deltaY = (Yp(linto(Linf)) - Yp(linfrom(Linf)))
                        m = 0: flg = 1
                        If deltaX = 0 Then GoTo 13 :'Gradient equal zero if dx=0
                        m = Abs(deltaY) / (deltaX): flg = 0
                        13 Yc = Yp(linfrom(linface(k, n)))
                        Xc = Xp(linfrom(linface(k, n)))
                        If Sgn(deltaY) < 0 Then m = m * -1
                        If m = 0 Then Xvalue(k) = Xc:  GoTo 87
                        Xvalue(k) = ((Yscan - Yc) / m) + Xc :'Equation of line
                        87 :'Repeat for all lines on face
                Next k
        'calc X value of center of scan line
            deltaX = (Xp(centface(n)) - xyminmax)
            deltaY = (Yp(centface(n)) - yto)
            m = 0: flg = 1
            If deltaX = 0 Then GoTo 131
            m = Abs(deltaY) / (deltaX): flg = 0
            131
            If Sgn(deltaY) < 0 Then m = m * -1
            If m = 0 Then Xvalue(k) = xyminmax: GoTo 871
            xcen = ((Yscan - yto) / m) + xyminmax
            871
            Xpmax = 10000# :'Reset max value of X
            Xpmin = -10000# :'Reset min value of X
            ps = 0: pps = 0
'Determine which X solutions are nearest the centre
            For k = 1 To 3
                Xdifn(k) = 0
                Xdifp(k) = 0
            Next k
            For k = 1 To 4
                pp = (Xvalue(k) - xcen)
                If pp < 0 Then ps = ps + 1: Xdifn(ps) = pp
                If pp > 0 Then pps = pps + 1: Xdifp(pps) = pp
            Next k
            For k = 1 To ps
                If Xdifn(k) > Xpmin Then Xpmin = Xdifn(k)
            Next k
            For k = 1 To pps
                If Xdifp(k) < Xpmax Then Xpmax = Xdifp(k)
            Next k
        'Draw fill line
        picture1.ForeColor = QBColor(1 + n)
picture1.Line (Xpmin + xcen + 3600, Yscan + 2700)-(Xpmax + xcen + 3600, Yscan + 2700)
Next Yscan
Next dd
End Sub
```

The painter's algorithm

Instead of determining which part of an obscured facet should be drawn it is simpler to use what is called the *painter's algorithm*. An artist will first paint the background then the most distant objects are painted on top. This procedure is continued until the closest foreground objects are painted on top of all the previous ones. By drawing the most distant facets and objects first then overdrawing those with the progressively closer objects, hidden facets and objects are automatically removed.

Figure 5.14
Solid cube
constructed
from filled
polygons

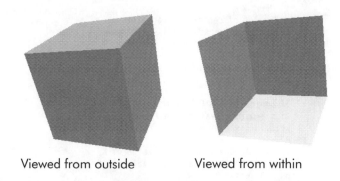

Viewed from outside   Viewed from within

We can use the methods described in the previous program example to determine which of the facets of an object are closest to the observer and by placing them in descending order, closest face first furthest face last, we have the drawing sequence. By reversing this drawing sequence we can also remove the front faces to allow us to look into objects as shown in Figure 5.14.

Chapter 6

Physical modelling

Through graphical modelling we have created the illusion of 3D on the screen, we will now develop a physical model of the behaviour of structures and materials.

Without physical laws or rules, geometric representations do not respond to or interact with each other or the environment: balls do not bounce when they hit the ground and objects pass through each other. Examples of falling with gravity; impact and restitution, and trajectories are used to demonstrate how the feeling of reality can be greatly enhanced when objects behave as expected. Techniques for interaction detection between objects are discussed and demonstrated using program examples. More advanced modelling of structures is achieved through the use of Finite Element Analysis allowing us to model the effect of the deformation of a ball as it is hit or hits an object or a membrane being pushed or pulled. Again these principles are demonstrated through program examples in open code allowing the more adventurous to explore the workings of a finite element modeller. Lastly the principles of object hierarchy are discussed where the relationship of objects is demonstrated using a simplified skeleton.

Physical modelling

Geometric representations of reality produce only a static 3D picture of the world. Though we can spin, scale and transform them the subject of the picture remains unchanged. As soon as we wish to animate the subject or scene then physical laws or rules are required. For example, in Figure 6.1 the geometric representation of a ball falls to the ground and bounces. An object travelling in the real world has mass and velocity; it is subject to gravity, air resistance and it collides with other objects. If these physical constraints are not included in our virtual world then the world looks and reacts falsely: objects move through each other, they do not fall to the ground or deform on impact. In the case of the dataglove, in order to provide force feedback from the virtual world, we need to calculate those forces which will allow us to feel the virtual world. We can however defy conventional physical laws and even invent new ones in a virtual world.

Figure 6.1
Bouncing ball

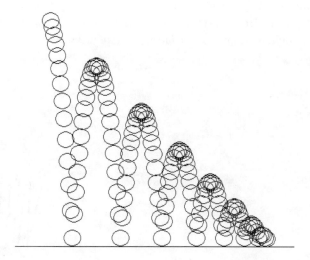

In this chapter we will describe examples of some basic physical laws, explain the need for interaction detection, and progress to advanced physical modelling using the finite element technique.

Falling with gravity

A bouncing ball

As Galileo discovered, when two balls of different mass are dropped from a high tower both balls hit the ground at the same time and, as Newton discovered, the reason objects fall towards the Earth is due to the force of gravity. To explain Galileo's observation: the two balls of differing mass are subject to the same acceleration due to the force of gravity; therefore, if they start at the same speed and accelerate at the same rate they will reach any distant point at the same time – provided no other forces act upon them.

If an object travels a set distance in a measured time then the speed (or more correctly the velocity) is described as the rate of change of displacement or the distance divided by the time. If an object is travelling with a set velocity and then changes to another velocity over a length of time then this is described as the rate of change of velocity or the *acceleration*.

During an impact between two objects the acceleration of the bodies decreases over a length of time, this is called the rate of change of acceleration or *impulse*.

If we take the example of the falling ball the initial velocity is zero, and the final velocity is zero, as it hits the ground. However in between these two states we can calculate the distance dropped at any time using the equation:

$$S = \tfrac{1}{2}gt^2$$

Where g is the acceleration due to gravity, S is the distance travelled and t is the duration. We can thus model a falling body by incrementing in small units of time and plotting the resultant displacement (S) on the Y-axis, as can be seen in the 'cannon' example program where the effects of adjusting the value of gravity can be observed.

The cannon ball example

In the cannon example program the ball is fired and exits the barrel with a certain velocity, the maximum height obtained by the ball is determined from the initial velocity and the counter effect of deceleration due to gravity. The vertical displacement is determined by the equation:

$$S_V = U_V - \frac{1}{2}gt^2$$

Where S_V is the vertical displacement and U_V is the initial vertical velocity. The horizontal displacement is determined by the equation:

$$S_h = U_h t$$

Where S_h is the horizontal displacement and U_h is the initial horizontal velocity.

We can fire the cannon at any angle between the vertical and horizontal, as we change the angle of the cannon so we change the proportion of horizontal to vertical velocity, which is determined from the 'cosine' and 'sine' functions of the muzzle velocity (exit velocity of the cannon ball). The horizontal displacement is not affected by gravity as it only acts in the vertical axis, thus the horizontal displacement is due to the initial horizontal ball velocity (assuming no air resistance).

The program cannon allows you to vary the angle of the cannon and you will find the ball will travel the maximum horizontal distance, before impact, when the angle is 45°, which is what happens in reality.

Motion of a cannon ball
program example

```
Sub bball ()
'cannon ball
    t = 0 :'Zero time
    sh = 0 :'Zero horizontal displacement
    sv = 0 :'Zero vertical displacement
    ti = .1 :'Time increments
    rb = 150 :'Radius of ball
    U = 300 :'Muzel Velocity
    gama = HScroll1.Value / 100 :'Set angle of trajectory
    g = -9.81 * (HScroll3.Value / 10) :'Set value of gravity
```

```
Do
    t = t + ti
    sh = (U * Cos(gama) * t) :'Horizontal displacement
    sv = ((U * Sin(gama)) * t) + (.5 * (g * (t ^ 2))) :'Vertical displacement
    color = QBColor(7)
    Circle (300 + sh, 5200 - sv), rb :'Draw ball
    Line (0, 5500)-(12000, 5500) :'Draw ground line
Loop
```

When the cannon ball hits the ground it would normally bury itself: thus the velocity after impact is zero. If, however, the ball was made of rubber we would expect it to bounce after impact. The ratio of the velocity before impact to the velocity after impact is known as the *coefficient of restitution* and its value is determined (via experiment) by the physical properties of the object and the contacted surface. In the program example we can vary the value of the coefficient and see the effect. The velocity after impact is set as the initial velocity, times the coefficient of restitution – as if the ball had been fired from a new cannon positioned at the impact site.

Impact and restitution
program example

```
10
sg = -100 :'Set ground height
cr = Hscroll2.Value / 100 :'Set coefficeint of restitution
travel = 0 :'Zero horizontal reposition
newstart = 0 :'Zero ground height reposition
Do
    t = t + ti
    sh = (U * Cos(gama) * t)
    sv = ((U * Sin(gama)) * t) + (.5 * (g * (t ^ 2)))
    If sh > 10000 Then Cls: sh = 0: GoTo 10 :'Reset when ball leaves the screen
    color = QBColor(7)
    Circle (300 + sh + travel, 5200 + newstart - sv), rb
    Line (0, 5500)-(12000, 5500)
    'interaction detection
    If sv < sg Then :'Is ball on or below ground level
            U = U * cr :'Calculate mew initial velocity
            t = 0 :'Reset time
            sg = 0 :'Reset ground height
            newstart = 110 :'Reposition cannon muzel at ground hieght
            travel = travel + sh :'Reposition cannon horizontal
    End If
Loop
End Sud
```

The combination of the angle of trajectory, acceleration due to gravity and the coefficient of restitution produce a physical model of the response of a virtual cannon ball when fired from a virtual cannon. The resultant values of displacement with time derived from physical laws are used to move the geometric representation of the ball which would otherwise remain stationary.

Interaction detection

In the previous example the presence of the ground causes the ball to impact and bounce but the equation which describes the motion of the ball does not take into account the ground. Indeed, if it were not there, as in the case of firing from a tower or cliff, the ball would fall below the launch point. So how is the presence of the ground determined?

Boundries and equations

In the previous cannon ball example the ground is set as horizontal displacement of zero. Thus, a rule is employed which says: if the value of displacement of the ball plus its radius becomes negative, then the ground has been contacted and the coefficient of restitution and the `refire` routine is run. This is an example of both interaction detection and an interaction rule.

In the example program titled `pool` a number of balls bounce inside a box colliding with the sides and each other. In order to determine if a ball has come into contact with a wall, and at which point on the circumference this occurred, we can compare the equation of the circumference of the ball with that of the equation of the line which represents the walls of the box. Thus, if at any point the equation of the circumference is equal to the equation of the line an interaction has occurred. In the pool-ball example, as the walls are perpendicular, it is sufficient to determine if a point on the circumference is greater or less than the lines X or Y position. The point on the circumference where the interaction occurred can be determined from the scan angle.

Ball–wall interaction: comparison of equations

program example

```
Sub ballWall
rb = 15 :'Set radius of ball
x = 100 :'Set initial ball position
theta = 135 :'Set initial angle of motion of ball
Cls
Do
    x = x + (SIN(theta / 57.3)) :'X coordinte of centre of ball
    y = y - (COS(theta / 57.3) * .72) :'Y coordinate of centre of ball
    Circle (20 + x, 150 + y), rb :'Draw ball
    Line (0, 1)-(600, 327), , b :'Draw wall
'Scan equation of circumference
For nn = 1 To 360 Step 45
    px = ((18) * SIN(nn / 57.3)) :'X coordinate value on circumference
    py = -1 * ((18) * COS(nn / 57.3)):'Y coordinate on circumference
'Interaction detection
    If (20 + px + x) > 600 Then :'Apply rule
    If (150 + (py * .72) + y) > 327 Then :'Apply rule
    If (20 + px + x) < 0 Then :'Apply rule
    if (150 + (py * .72) + y) < 1 Then :'Apply rule
    Next nn
Loop
End Sub
```

Another method of interaction detection which can be used is that of expansion and contraction of objects. In the case of ball-to-ball interactions the circumference of one ball is expanded by the addition of the radius of the ball to be checked. Then it is simply a case of checking to see if the centre point of the checked ball lies within the circumference of the other. As shown in Figure 6.2, interaction is detected when the distance between both ball centres is less than the value of the their combined radii. This sequence is repeated with the main balls being checked against each other to determine if interaction has occurred. The next ball is then compared with every other ball, and this is repeated until all balls have been checked against each other.

Figure 6.2
Interaction checking of spheres

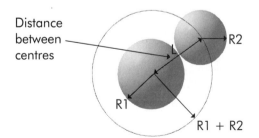

Distance between centres

R2

R1

R1 + R2

Though this method is fairly fast and simple it is not possible to model virtual worlds entirely from circles, and as we have seen from previous chapters most geometric modellers use polygons as the geometric primitive. We can apply the same interaction principle to polygons, cubes or tubes by first reducing them to a 2D representation by expanding the checking object by the Z-dimension thus reducing them to polygons. The polygon can then be reduced to a line by subtracting the width or breadth and expanding the checking object. Lastly, the checked object is reduced to a point by expanding the object by the length in that axis, as shown in Figure 6.3.

Figure 6.3
Interaction detection expansion and reduction

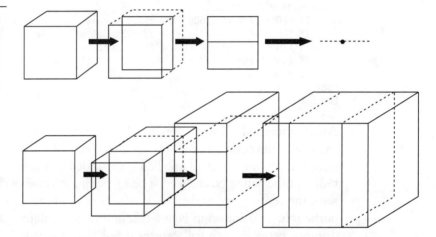

It is then just a matter of checking to see if the reduced point object is within the expanded object by comparing the distance to the surface of the object from its centre and the distance between the two centres as in the ball example.

Ball–ball interaction expansion/ reduction
program example

```
Sub pball ()
noball = 1:'Set number of balls
    ReDim xt(noball), yt(noball), Xdif(noball), rd(noball), bttheta(noball),
    tttheta(noball)
    rd(1) = 150 :'Set radius of ball
    bttheta(1) = 135 :'Initial angle of motion of ball
    Xdif(1) = 0 :'Offset position from orogin of ball
Do
'Draw ball and Wall
    picture1.Cls
    For tn = 1 To noball
        tttheta(tn) = bttheta(tn)
```

```
        xt(tn) = xt(tn) + (50 * (Sin(tttheta(tn) / 57.3)))
        yt(tn) = yt(tn) - (50 * (Cos(tttheta(tn) / 57.3)))
        picture1.ForeColor = QBColor(0)
        picture1.Line (100, 100)-(6080, 3000), , B :'Draw walls
'Draw balls
        picture1.Circle (2000 + Xdif(tn) + xt(tn), 1500 + yt(tn)), rd(tn)
Next tn

'Ball-wall interaction detection
For n = 1 To noball
        If (2000 + Xdif(n) + rd(n) + xt(n)) > 6030 Then :'If ballApply rule
        If (2000 + Xdif(n) - rd(n) + xt(n)) < 150 Then :'Apply rule
        If (1500 - rd(n) + yt(n)) < 150 Then :'Apply rule
        If (1500 + rd(n) + yt(n)) > 2950 Then :'Apply rule

'Ball-ball interaction detection
For t = 1 To noball
    leg = Sqr((((Xdif(n)+xt(n))-(Xdif(t)+xt(t))) ^ 2)+((yt(n)-yt(t)) ^ 2))
    If leg < (rd(n) + rd(t)) Then :' Apply rule
Next t
Next n
Loop
End Sub
```

The effect of interaction detection can be seen in pool by turning off
either the wall or ball interaction detectors which cause the balls either
to escape the container or to travel through each other.

Figure 6.4
Incident
reflection as an
interaction rule

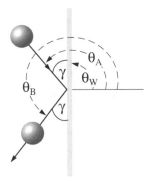

Once an interaction between objects is detected then a rule or physical
law is applied to produce a realistic response. In the case of ball–wall
interactions once detected the law of incident reflection is applied, see
Figure 6.4, in which the angle of collision equals the angle of incidence.

In order to determine the angle after collision we require additional information about the wall's angle and the ball's trajectory. The angle of trajectory of the ball is held as a variable and the angle of the wall can be calculated from the co-ordinates of its start and finish points. Thus the angle of trajectory after impact can be derived from the equation:

$$\theta_A = \theta_B + 2(\theta_W - \theta_B)$$

Where θ_B is the angle of the ball before impact, θ_A is the angle after impact and θ_W is the angle of the wall (shown in Figure 6.4).

Figure 6.5
Ball–ball
collision rule

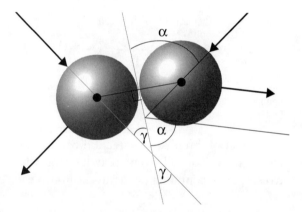

Similarly, when a ball–ball interaction is detected a different version of the incident reflection rule is applied. Once the trajectory angles of the two balls have been looked-up, and the point/angle of contact of the two balls has been calculated, as shown in Figure 6.5. The resultant incident angles of the two balls can be calculated from the previous wall equation. The wall angle is calculated by placing an imaginary wall perpendicular to the contact point of the two balls.

Incident reflection interaction rule
program example

```
'check walls
If (xt(n)+rd(n)> 6030 Then bttheta(n)= bttheta(n)+2*(180-bttheta(n)):hit= 1
If (xt(n)-rd(n))< 150 Then bttheta(n)= bttheta(n)+2*(180-bttheta(n)):hit= 1
If (yt(n)-rd(n))< 150 Then bttheta(n)= bttheta(n)+ 2*(90- bttheta(n)):hit= 1
If (yt(n)+rd(n))> 2950 Then bttheta(n)= bttheta(n)+2*(90-bttheta(n)): hit= 1

'Ball/ball interaction
'Calculate distance between centres
leg = Sqr(((Xdif(n)+xt(n)) - (Xdif(t) + xt(t))) ^ 2) + ((yt(n) - yt(t)) ^ 2))
thetaw = ((Atn(((Xdif(n)+xt(n)) - (Xdif(t)+xt(t))) / (yt(n) - yt(t))) * 57.3))
```

```
'Compare with sum of radii
If leg < (rd(n) + rd(t)) Then
'Apply rule
bttheta(n) = tttheta(n) + 2 * ((270 - thetaw) - tttheta(n))
bttheta(t) = tttheta(t) + 2 * ((270 - thetaw) - tttheta(t))
```

Advanced physical modelling

The simple equations of the laws of motion, discussed earlier, are unable to describe complex motions which arise in such situations as the deformation of a membrane or aircraft structure or the flow of particles round a complex shape. Although, in some instances, a single equation can be derived to describe events, they are usually specific to the case. For instance, the deformation response of a beam due to a load applied at its centre can be summarised in a single simple equation:

$$d = \frac{PL^3}{192EI}$$

Where d is the deflection, L is the length of the beam, P is the applied load, E is the stiffness of the beam and I is a measure of the cross-sectional structural stiffness of the beam.

As the number and variety of loads increase so the equation complexity increases. When the material shape and interactions becomes too complex (ie for large deflections) the underlying assumptions of the equations no longer hold true. In order to solve this problem and allow us to model more complex systems the finite element method was developed.

Finite element (FE) analysis method

Finite element methods were first developed for applications in aeronautical and civil engineering in the late 1940s and early 1950s where they were used to solve structural design problems. With the increase in the size of memory and processing power of computers so the areas of application increased to include thermal, vibration and fluid problems.

The FE method involves the division of a physical system into a series of small sub systems or elements. Each element can be treated as a simple unit whose behaviour is well explained with proven theories and equations. Each element is joined to its neighbour at nodes which are common to both. Individual elements are related to each other by the assemblage of a series of differential equations which represent each element. Thus a number of identical elements using, say, simple beam theory can model the effects of both a curved beam and a cantilever beam under any combination of loading conditions and constraints.

It is easiest to describe the principles of FE by considering a simple problem of springs connected in series. Figure 6.6 shows a simple setup where K_a and K_b are the spring stiffness constants and 1, 2, 3 are the nodes at which loads P_1, P_2 and P_3 are the internal spring forces and U_1, U_2 and U_3 are the nodal displacements.

Figure 6.6
Simple spring
elements

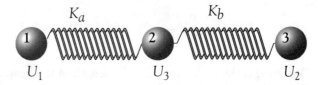

Each spring will be considered separately, then by considering an equilibrium state the equations relating the springs can be obtained.

Case 1
Node 1 has displacement of U_1, nodes 2 and 3 are fixed. As the force (P) to extend a spring is given by the equation $P = K \times$ *extension of spring*, the load at node 1 can be defined as:

$$P_1 = K_a(U_1 - U_2) \text{ as } U_2 = 0, \text{ then } P_1 = K_a U_1$$

Node 2 must provide an equal but opposite force for equilibrium, (no displacement at node 2), thus $P_2^1 = -K_a U_1$.

Case 2
Node 2 has a displacement of U_2, nodes 1 and 3 are fixed. As for case 1, the equilibrium load at node 2 due to the first spring, (P_2^1) and the equilibrium load due to the second spring, (P_2^2) are equal and opposite;

thus:

$$P_1 = K_a(U_1 - U_2) = K_a(0 - U_2) \text{ thus } P_1 = -K_a U_2$$
$$P_3 = K_b(U_3 - U_2) = K_b(0 - U_2) \text{ thus } P_3 = -K_b U_2$$

Case 3

Node 3 has a displacement of U_3, nodes 1 and 2 are fixed, thus:

$$P_3 = K_b(U_3 - U_2) \text{ as } U_2 = 0 \text{ then } P_3 = K_b U_3$$
$$P_2^2 = -P_3 \text{ as } K_b U_3 \text{ then } P_2^2 = -K_b U_3$$
$$P_2^1 = -P_1 = K_a U_2 \text{ thus } P_2^1 = K_a U_2$$
$$P_2^2 = -P_3 = K_b U_2 \text{ thus } P_2^2 = K_b U_2$$

We must now consider the structure with all three displacements simultaneously to determine the overall structure relationship. This can be done by superimposing cases 1, 2 and 3:

$$P_1 = K_a U_1 - K_a U_2$$
$$P_3 = K_b U_3 - K_b U_2$$
$$P_2 = (K_a + K_b)U_2 - K_b U_3 - K_a U_1$$

There are now 3 simultaneous equations which can be represented in matrix form:

$$\begin{Bmatrix} P_1 \\ P_2 \\ P_3 \end{Bmatrix} = \begin{bmatrix} K_a & -K_a & 0 \\ -K_a & (K_a + K_b) & -K_b \\ 0 & -K_b & K_b \end{bmatrix} \begin{Bmatrix} U_1 \\ U_2 \\ U_3 \end{Bmatrix}$$

In finite element terms $\{P\}$ is the load vector, $[K]$ is the structural stiffness matrix and $\{U_i\}$ is the displacement vector.

$$\{U\} = [K]^{-1}\{P\}$$

In order to solve these simultaneous equations, to provide a force–displacement relationship, the values of the constraints of the structure

Chapter 6

must be input. As the structure is floating in space we must constrain at least one node. If the value of the loads at each node is now input we have 4 constraints leaving 3 displacements as unknowns. The matrix can therefore be solved as we have one more equation than we do unknowns.

As can be seen from the previous example even this simple problem requires considerable computation due to the large number of iterative loops involved in setting up and solving the matrices.

The previous example only considers the elastic bending case. In order to include plastic deformation a second stiffness matrix has to be formed known as a materials compensation matrix. It is formed in the same way as the structure stiffness matrix and the two matrices are added together. Stiffness increases, due to changes in geometry and this can also be included by generating a geometric compensation matrix and adding this to both of the previous matrices.

Although this method is capable of modelling a large variety of shapes and variations, it requires considerable computational power to construct and solve the matrices of simultaneous equations. For more information on the FE method the readers attention is drawn to *Finite Element Methods in Engineering Science* by C T F Ross, published by Ellis Horwood.

We have written a simple FE package which is included in uncompiled format running under *DOS* through *QuickBasic*. This has been converted to run under *Windows* as demonstration programs. The first, shown in Figure 6.7, shows a beam which is fixed at one end whilst the other is subjected to a twisting moment. The effect is like that of rolling up a newspaper, the tightness of the twist is determined by the stiffness of the material. By adjusting the stiffness in the model, by increasing or decreasing the value of the variable Emoduel within the FE package set-up routine, the beam can be made to fold within itself as if you were opening a tin of ham or corned beef.

Figure 6.7
Paper rolling
example

The next demonstration shows how the same package can be used to model the response of a ball hitting a wall, as shown in Figure 6.8. In this case the interaction–detection techniques described earlier are used to determine when and where the impact has occurred. This information is used to generate the nodal constraints and loads required to solve the finite element problem. The shape of the model is determined by setting the element node positions. In the case of the beam example this is generated by indexing the new node position by the element length, recording the X and Y co-ordinates, until the required beam length is obtained. In the ball example, the equation of a circle is used to generate the nodal positions. By specifying the node coordinates in the open version of the FE package it is possible create your own structures.

Figure 6.8
FE ball hitting
wall

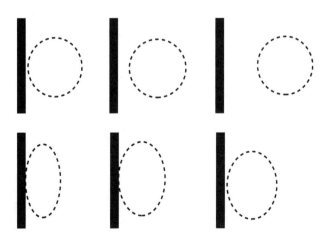

In the third example, a semicircular membrane is generated which is then loaded at subsequent nodes. The structure deflects to a greater or lesser extent dependent on where it is loaded – which is due to the geometric structural strength. As can be seen when the structure is loaded from the side it starts to collapse whereas when loaded nearer the top with the same load the structure deflects only slightly. Indeed, when loaded at the top there is no noticeable deflection so at this point a negative load or pull is applied to show that the structural strength is directional.

Figure 6.9
Membrane structure under load

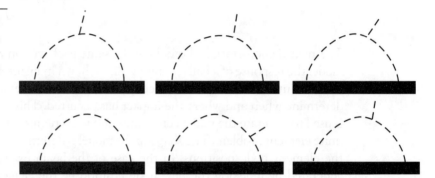

The FE modelling technique can also determine the stresses within the structure and hence the reaction forces; thus if the loads are applied to the FE model by the virtual hand through the dataglove the reaction forces can be used to provide the information for realistic force feedback.

Setting node position and constraints
program example

```
Sub Basques ()
ReDim x(22), y(22)
'Genteratate nodal coordinates
'Ball
For hj = 90 To 469 Step 18
    f = f + 1
    x(f) = 20 + (60 + 25 * (Sin(hj / 57.3)))
    y(f) = (40 + 25 * (Cos(hj / 57.3)))
Next hj
'Or Beam
    x(1) = 44: x(2) = 48: x(3) = 52: x(4) = 56: x(5) = 60
    x(6) = 64: x(7) = 68: x(8) = 72: x(9) = 76: x(10) = 80
    x(11) = 84: x(12) = 88: x(13) = 92: x(14) = 96: x(15) = 100
    x(16) = 104: x(17) = 108: x(18) = 112: x(19) = 116: x(20) = 120
    y(1) = 20: y(2) = 20: y(3) = 20: y(4) = 20: y(5) = 20
    y(6) = 20: y(7) = 20: y(8) = 20: y(9) = 20: y(10) = 20
    y(11) = 20: y(12) = 20: y(13) = 20: y(14) = 20: y(15) = 20
    y(16) = 20: y(17) = 20: y(18) = 20: y(19) = 20: y(20) = 20
    ls = 20: 'no. elements
    NF = 3: 'no. fixed nodes
    nc = 1: 'no.loaded nodes
```

```
    NW = 6: 'Width of beam matrix
    NN = (ls + 1) * 3: 'No of load coordinates
    ReDim NS(NF * 3), qc(NN), elemodu(ls)
For i = 1 To ls
    elemodu(i) = 26271
Next i
'Fix node data
    NS(1) = 1
    NS(2) = 2
    NS(3) = 3
'Set load data
    qc(60) = -8

'**** RUN FE ENGINE ****
```

We have used the finite element method to produce a physical model of the response of strip metal to the actions of a virtual manufacturing system shown in Figure 6.10. This sequence shows raw material being formed into shape to produce a virtual component which, as it is a physical model, can be used to test the response of the part.

Figure 6.10
Virtual
manufacturing
sequence

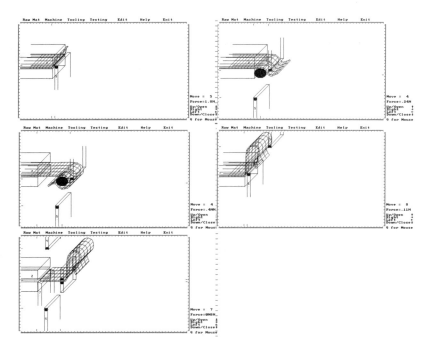

Moving objects

Object hierarchy

If we take the example of a ball placed on a perspective grid shown in Figure 6.11 it can be seen that as the size of the ball increases or decreases it appears to move away or towards the viewer. By changing the radius of the circle we can move along the Z-axis into and out of the screen. To move the ball to the left or right we merely increment or decrement the X (horizontal screen axis) axis of the origin of the ball. Similarly we can move up and down by indexing the Y-axis of the object. The program example below demonstrates the motion control of a ball through cursor key input with the addition of U and D keys to control the third axis.

Figure 6.11
Ball moving on
virtual plane

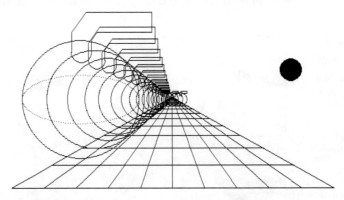

Moving a ball
program
example

```
'motionofball
in$=INKEY$
'into-outofscreenZaxis
    IF in$=CHR$(0)+CHR$(80)THEN m=m+((4*n/40)*(m/n)):n=n+(4*n/40)
    IF in$=CHR$(0)+CHR$(72)THEN m=m-((4*n/40)*(m/n)):n=n-(4*n/40)
'left-right
    IF in$=CHR$(0)+CHR$(77)THEN m=m+(4*n/40)
    IF in$=CHR$(0)+CHR$(75)THEN m=m-(4*n/40)
'up-down
    IF in$="u"THENzzz=zzz+2
    IF in$="d"THENzzz=zzz-2
    CIRCLE(ox+m,oy-ss+zzz),(2+n)
in$=""
```

As an object moves out of the screen so the step size, along the Z-axis, increases and the object appears to accelerate towards you; as the object moves away into the screen so the step sizes decreases and the object appears to decelerate never quite reaching the horizon line.

Relating objects

In the previous example the motion of the ball was controlled through the keyboard, this can be replaced by the positional data generated from the dataglove and hand tracker allowing, for example, a representation of a finger to be moved in 3D. If we now want to use this virtual finger to move other objects such as the ball then we need to determine when these objects are in contact and in which direction collision occurred. Using the interaction detection techniques described in the *Interaction detection* section (starting on page 82) we can determine when and where the contact between finger and ball has occurred. If the finger contacts the ball then the ball should roll with the finger, but if the finger then moves away from the ball then they should separate and the ball remain stationary.

3D interaction detection

program example

```
'interaction detection
'zaxis position of finger
    Zfing = INT(nnn * 1.338)
'zaxis position of ball
    Zball = INT(n)
'interaction pixel coordinates on ball
    top = (ox + mmm)
    ball = (oy - ss) - (2 + ((nnn / 2) * 1.35))
    switch$ = "y"
```

In addition to interaction detection we require a rule set which will join the motions of the finger and ball together, with the motion of the ball being that of the finger provided that the finger is moving towards the centre of the ball. In relationship terms we say that the finger is the parent of the ball.

Interaction rules

program example

```
'interaction rules
'Is the finger on the ball
IF POINT(top, ball) = 0 THEN switch$ = "n": GOTO 24
IF Zfing <> Zball THEN switch$ = "n" :' is finger behind ball
'Link motion of finger and ball
IF Zfing = Zball + 1 OR Zfing = Zball - 1 THEN switch$ = "y"
```

Chapter 6

```
                    'Link motion of finger and ball
                    IF Zball = Zfing + 1 OR Zball = Zfing - 1 THEN switch$ = "y"
                    24
```

MOVEBALL
program

```
DECLARE SUB movefinger ()
DECLARE SUB moveball ()
'set variables
DIM SHARED nohoz, nover, ss, erh, ssa, ssm, erv, ssam
DIM SHARED sss, ssp, ox, oy, ns, beta, n, m, nnn, mmm
DIM SHARED sins, spin, savp, jmp$, w, b, aspectw, sav
DIM SHARED startp, endp, yonk, switch$, zzz
apage = 0: vpage = 1
nohoz = 20: nover = 5
ss = 120: erh = .25: ssa = ss - (ss * erh)
ssm = 400: erv = .25: ssam = (ssm * erv)
sss = 60: ssp = -sss
ox = 320: oy = 260: ns = 4
beta = .35
'motion
sins = 1: spin = 0: savp = 0: jmp$ = "s"
w = 2: b = 2: aspectw = 1: sav = 1
'circle routine
startp = 1: endp = 150: yonk = endp / (2 * 3.14)
DO
SCREEN 9, , apage, vpage
VIEW (1, 1)-(638, 338), 0, 5
COLOR 2, 0
COLOR 15
'moon
CIRCLE (540, 100), 20
PAINT (557, 100)
COLOR 5
'Draw horizontal grid lines
FOR t = 0 TO nohoz
'line spacing
ss = ss - (ss * erh) - ssa
'line length
ssm = ssm - (ssm * erv)
LINE (ox - ssm, oy + (ss * SIN(beta)))-(ox, oy + (ss * SIN(beta)))
LINE (ox + ssm, oy + (ss * SIN(beta)))-(ox, oy + (ss * SIN(beta)))
NEXT t
'draw vertical grid lines
FOR t = 0 TO nover
'line length equals height
ssp = ssp + sss
LINE (ox, oy + (ss * SIN(beta)))-(ox + ssp, oy)
LINE (ox, oy + (ss * SIN(beta)))-(ox - ssp, oy)
NEXT t
'reset counters
ss = 120
ssm = 400
```

```
sss = 60
ssp = -60
IF n < 2 THEN n = 2
IF nnn < 2 THEN nnn = 2
sav = spin
savp = aspectw
'motion of finger
in$ = INKEY$
IF in$=CHR$(0)+CHR$(80)THEN m=m+((4*n/40)*(m/n)):n=n+(4*n/40)
IF in$=CHR$(0)+CHR$(72)THEN m=m-((4*n/40)*(m/n)):n=n-(4*n/40)
IF in$=CHR$(0)+CHR$(77)THEN m=m+(4*n/40)
IF in$=CHR$(0)+CHR$(75)THEN m=m-(4*n/40)
IF in$="u"THENzzz=zzz+2
IF in$="d"THENzzz=zzz-2
CIRCLE(ox+m,oy-ss+zzz),(2+n)
in$=""
'motionofball
IF switch$="n"THEN GOTO 23
IF jmp$="k"THEN mmm=mmm+(4*nnn/40):aspectw=spin/.72:spin=savp*.72
:jmp$="s":in$="s"
IF jmp$="h"THEN mmm=mmm-(4*nnn/40):spin=.72*aspectw:aspectw=sav/.72
:jmp$="s":in$="s"
IF in$=CHR$(0)+CHR$(80)THEN mmm=mmm+((4*nnn/40)*(mmm/nnn)):nnn=nnn+(4*nnn/
40):spin=spin+(.3*sins)
IF in$=CHR$(0)+CHR$(72)THEN mmm=mmm-((4*nnn/40)*(mmm/nnn)):nnn=nnn-(4*nnn/
40):spin=spin+(.3*sins)
IF in$=CHR$(0)+CHR$(77)THEN mmm=mmm+(4*nnn/40):aspectw=spin/.72
:spin=savp*.72:jmp$="k"
IF in$=CHR$(0)+CHR$(75)THEN mmm=mmm-(4*nnn/40):spin=.72*aspectw:aspectw=sav/
.72:jmp$="h"
IF spin > .5 THEN sins = -1
IF spin < .2 THEN sins = 1
23
CALL movefinger
'interaction detection
Zfing = INT(nnn * 1.338)
Zball = INT(n)
top = (ox + mmm)
ball = (oy - ss) - (2 + ((nnn / 2) * 1.35))
switch$ = "y"
IF POINT(top, ball) = 0 THEN switch$ = "n": GOTO 24
IF Zfing <> Zball THEN switch$ = "n"
IF Zfing = Zball + 1 OR Zfing = Zball - 1 THEN switch$ = "y"
IF Zball = Zfing + 1 OR Zball = Zfing - 1 THEN switch$ = "y"
24 in$ = " "
CALL moveball
SWAP apage, vpage
LOOP
SUB moveball
COLOR 14
'circle inner
```

Chapter 6

```
           FOR nn = startp TO endp
           x = ((w + nnn) * SIN(nn / yonk)) * aspectw
           y = ((b + nnn) * COS(nn / yonk)) * spin
           PSET (ox + x + mmm, oy + y - ss)
           NEXT nn
           'circle outer
           CIRCLE (ox + mmm, oy - ss), (2 + nnn)
           END SUB
           SUB movefinger
           hh = -.15
           COLOR 3
LINE (ox+m+n-(n*.9),oy-ss+(n+zzz)-((n+zzz)*(2.25+hh)))-(ox+m+n+(n*.25),oy-ss+(n+zzz)-((n+zzz)*(2.25+hh)))
LINE (ox+m+n-(n*.7),oy-ss-(n+zzz)-((n+zzz)*(0+hh)))-(ox+m+n+(n*.25),oy-ss-(n+zzz)-((n+zzz)*(0+hh)))
LINE (ox+m+n-(n*.9),oy-ss+(n+zzz)-((n+zzz)*(2.25+hh)))-(ox+m+n-(n*1.15),oy-ss-(n+zzz)-((n+zzz)*(0+hh)))
LINE (ox+m+n-(n*1.15),oy-ss+(n+zzz)-((n+zzz)*(1.75+hh)))-(ox+m+n-(n*1.15),oy-ss-(n+zzz)-((n+zzz)*(0+hh)))
LINE (ox+m+n-(n*.7),oy-ss-(n+zzz)-((n+zzz)*(0+hh)))-(ox+m+n-(n*.8),oy-ss+(n+zzz)-((n+zzz)*(1.9+hh)))
LINE (ox+m+n-(n*.8),oy-ss+(n+zzz)+((n+zzz)*(.25-hh)))-(ox+m+n-(n*.8),oy-ss+(n+zzz)-((n+zzz)*(1.9+hh)))
LINE (ox+m+n+(n*.25),oy-ss+(n+zzz)-((n+zzz)*(2.25+hh)))-(ox+m+n+(n*.25),oy-ss-(n+zzz)-((n+zzz)*(0+hh)))
CIRCLE (ox+m+n-(n*.975),oy-ss-(n+zzz)+((n+zzz)*(.25-hh))),(n*.175),,3.14,0
PAINT (ox+m+n-(n*.975),oy-ss-(n+zzz)+((n+zzz)*(.25-hh)))
           END SUB
```

Hierarchical data structures

As shown previously we can relate objects together so that as we move one we move the other. There is also a hierarchy in that some objects may move others – ie the finger moves the ball but the ball cannot move the finger: the finger is said to be the parent of the ball. If we take the example of a person shown in Figure 6.12, the body is the parent and it has five children: two arms, two legs and one head. If we move the body all the children must also move by the same displacement. The children of the body can themselves be parents, the arm has a child called the hand and the leg has a child call the foot. If we move the leg or arm then the foot or hand must also move. Moving the body will move all its children and its grandchildren whereas moving a child or grandchild will not move the body.

The components which make up the person are stored in hierarchical order from parent to child and on through the generations. The program example allows you to move the various parts of the person to see this relationship. It is also possible to include rules which change this relationship, for instance if the person is pulled by the arm then the arm becomes the parent of the body and the whole person moves.

Figure 6.12
Stick man body
part hierarchy

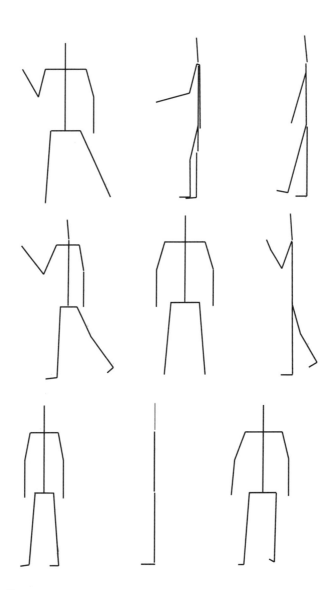

**Hierarchical
data structure**
program
example

```
'Setup Man
Nobjects = 19 :'No Lines
'Set Arrays
DIM  Name$(Nobjects), obj(Nobjects, 8), x(Nobjects), y(Nobjects),z(Nobjects)


'Initial Conditions,  Parent Object, Length Object, Delta, Gamma
Name$(1)="World": obj(1,1)=0: obj(1,2)=0: obj(1,3)=0/57.3: ob(1,4)=0/57.3
```

```
'End coordinates
obj(1, 6) = 0 + (obj(1, 2) * COS(obj(1, 4)) * COS(obj(1, 3))) :'X
obj(1, 7) = 0 + (obj(1, 2) * COS(obj(1, 4)) * COS(obj(1, 3))) :'Y
obj(1, 8) = 0 + (obj(1, 2) * SIN(obj(1, 4))) :'Z

'First Generation
Name$(2)="Body"
obj(2,1)=1: obj(2,2)=100: obj(2,3)=(90/57.3) + obj(1,3): obj(2,4)=(0/57.3) + obj(1,4)
obj(2, 6) = obj(1, 6) + (obj(2, 2) * COS(obj(1, 4)) * COS(obj(2, 3))):
obj(2, 7) = obj(1, 7) + (obj(2, 2) * COS(obj(1, 4)) * SIN(obj(2, 3))):
obj(2, 8) = obj(1, 8) + (obj(2, 2) * SIN(obj(2, 4)))

'Second Generation
Name$(3) = "HipL"
obj(3,1)=2: obj(3,2)=25: obj(3,3)=(90/57.3) + obj(2,3): obj(3, 4) = (0 / 57.3) + obj(2, 4)
obj(3, 6) = obj(2, 6) + (obj(3, 2) * COS(obj(3, 4)) * COS(obj(3, 3)))
obj(3, 7) = obj(2, 7) + (obj(3, 2) * COS(obj(3, 4)) * SIN(obj(3, 3)))
obj(3, 8) = obj(2, 8) + (obj(3, 2) * SIN(obj(3, 4)))
Name$(4) = "HipR"
obj(4,1)=2: obj(4,2)=25: obj(4,3)=(-90/57.3) + obj(2,3): obj(4,4)=(0/57.3) + obj(2,4)
obj(4, 6) = obj(2, 6) + (obj(4, 2) * COS(obj(4, 4)) * COS(obj(4, 3)))
obj(4, 7) = obj(2, 7) + (obj(4, 2) * COS(obj(4, 4)) * SIN(obj(4, 3)))
obj(4, 8) = obj(2, 8) + (obj(4, 2) * SIN(obj(4, 4)))
Name$(7) = "ShldR"
obj(7,1)=1: obj(7,2)=35: obj(7,3)=(90/57.3) + obj(2,3): obj(7,4)=(5/57.3) + obj(2,4)
obj(7, 6) = obj(1, 6) + (obj(7, 2) * COS(obj(7, 4)) * COS(obj(7, 3)))
obj(7, 7) = obj(1, 7) + (obj(7, 2) * COS(obj(7, 4)) * SIN(obj(7, 3)))
obj(7, 8) = obj(2, 8) + (obj(7, 2) * SIN(obj(7, 4)))
Name$(8) = "ShldL"
obj(8,1)=1: obj(8,2)=35: obj(8,3)=(-90/57.3) + obj(2,3): obj(8,4)=(0/57.3) + obj(2,4)
obj(8, 6) = obj(1, 6) + (obj(8, 2) * COS(obj(8, 4)) * COS(obj(8, 3)))
obj(8, 7) = obj(1, 7) + (obj(8, 2) * COS(obj(8, 4)) * SIN(obj(8, 3)))
obj(8, 8) = obj(2, 8) + (obj(8, 2) * SIN(obj(8, 4)))
Name$(9) = "Head"
obj(9,1)=1: obj(9,2)=45: obj(9,3)=(180/57.3) + obj(2,3): obj(9,4)=(5/57.3) + obj(2,4)
obj(9, 6) = obj(1, 6) + (obj(9, 2) * COS(obj(9, 4)) * COS(obj(9, 3)))
obj(9, 7) = obj(1, 7) + (obj(9, 2) * COS(obj(9, 4)) * SIN(obj(9, 3)))
obj(9, 8) = obj(2, 8) + (obj(9, 2) * SIN(obj(9, 4)))

'Third Generation
Name$(5) = "ULegL"
obj(5,1)=4: obj(5,2)=60: obj(5,3)=(65/57.3) + obj(4,3): obj(5,4)=(-15/57.3) + obj(3,4)
obj(5, 6) = obj(4, 6) + (obj(5, 2) * COS(obj(5, 4)) * COS(obj(5, 3)))
obj(5, 7) = obj(4, 7) + (obj(5, 2) * COS(obj(5, 4)) * SIN(obj(5, 3)))
obj(5, 8) = obj(3, 8) + (obj(5, 2) * SIN(obj(5, 4)))
Name$(6) = "ULegR"
obj(6,1)=3: obj(6,2)=60: obj(6,3)=(-85/57.3) + obj(3,3): obj(6,4)=(0/57.3) + obj(4,4)
obj(6, 6) = obj(3, 6) + (obj(6, 2) * COS(obj(6, 4)) * COS(obj(6, 3)))
obj(6, 7) = obj(3, 7) + (obj(6, 2) * COS(obj(6, 4)) * SIN(obj(6, 3)))
obj(6, 8) = obj(4, 8) + (obj(6, 2) * SIN(obj(6, 4)))
```

```
Name$(10) = "UArmR"
obj(10,1)=7: obj(10,2)=50: obj(10,3)=(-75/57.3) + obj(7,3): obj(10,4)=(15/57.3) + obj(7,4)
obj(10, 6) = obj(7, 6) + (obj(10, 2) * COS(obj(10, 4)) * COS(obj(10, 3)))
obj(10, 7) = obj(7, 7) + (obj(10, 2) * COS(obj(10, 4)) * SIN(obj(10, 3)))
obj(10, 8) = obj(7, 8) + (obj(10, 2) * SIN(obj(10, 4)))
Name$(11) = "UArmL"
obj(11,1)=8: obj(11,2)=50: obj(11,3)=(75/57.3) + obj(8,3): obj(11,4)=(0/57.3) + obj(8,4)
obj(11, 6) = obj(8, 6) + (obj(11, 2) * COS(obj(11, 4)) * COS(obj(11, 3)))
obj(11, 7) = obj(8, 7) + (obj(11, 2) * COS(obj(11, 4)) * SIN(obj(11, 3)))
obj(11, 8) = obj(8, 8) + (obj(11, 2) * SIN(obj(11, 4)))

'Fourth Generation
Name$(12) = "LArmR"
obj(12,1)=10:obj(12,2)=40:obj(12,3)=(-45/57.3)+obj(10,3): obj(12,4)=(130/57.3)+obj(10, 4)
obj(12, 6) = obj(10, 6) + (obj(12, 2) * COS(obj(12, 4)) * COS(obj(12, 3)))
obj(12, 7) = obj(10, 7) + (obj(12, 2) * COS(obj(12, 4)) * SIN(obj(12, 3)))
obj(12, 8) = obj(10, 8) + (obj(12, 2) * SIN(obj(12, 4)))
Name$(13) = "LArmL"
obj(13,1)=11: obj(13,2)=40: obj(13,3)=(15/57.3)+obj(11,3): obj(13,4)=(0/57.3)+obj(11,4)
obj(13, 6) = obj(11, 6) + (obj(13, 2) * COS(obj(13, 4)) * COS(obj(13, 3)))
obj(13, 7) = obj(11, 7) + (obj(13, 2) * COS(obj(13, 4)) * SIN(obj(13, 3)))
obj(13, 8) = obj(11, 8) + (obj(13, 2) * SIN(obj(13, 4)))
Name$(16) = "LLegL"
obj(16,1)=5: obj(16,2)=60: obj(16,3)=(0/57.3) + obj(5,3): obj(16,4)=(-15/57.3) + obj(5, 4)
obj(16, 6) = obj(5, 6) + (obj(16, 2) * COS(obj(16, 4)) * COS(obj(16, 3)))
obj(16, 7) = obj(5, 7) + (obj(16, 2) * COS(obj(16, 4)) * SIN(obj(16, 3)))
obj(16, 8) = obj(5, 8) + (obj(16, 2) * SIN(obj(16, 4)))
Name$(17) = "LLegR"
obj(17,1)=6: obj(17,2)=60: obj(17,3)=(0/57.3) + obj(6,3): obj(17,4)=(0/57.3) + obj(6,4)
obj(17, 6) = obj(6, 6) + (obj(17, 2) * COS(obj(17, 4)) * COS(obj(17, 3)))
obj(17, 7) = obj(6, 7) + (obj(17, 2) * COS(obj(17, 4)) * SIN(obj(17, 3)))
obj(17, 8) = obj(6, 8) + (obj(17, 2) * SIN(obj(17, 4)))

'Fifth Generation
Name$(14) = "HandR"
obj(14,1)=12: obj(14,2)=20: obj(14,3)=(0/57.3)+obj(12,3): obj(14,4)=(10/57.3)+obj(12,4)
obj(14, 6) = obj(12, 6) + (obj(14, 2) * COS(obj(14, 4)) * COS(obj(14, 3)))
obj(14, 7) = obj(12, 7) + (obj(14, 2) * COS(obj(14, 4)) * SIN(obj(14, 3)))
obj(14, 8) = obj(12, 8) + (obj(14, 2) * SIN(obj(14, 4)))
Name$(15) = "HandL"
obj(15,1)=13: obj(15,2)=20: obj(15,3)=(0/57.3) + obj(13,3): obj(15,4)=(0/57.3) + obj(13,4)
obj(15, 6) = obj(13, 6) + (obj(15, 2) * COS(obj(15, 4)) * COS(obj(15, 3)))
obj(15, 7) = obj(13, 7) + (obj(15, 2) * COS(obj(15, 4)) * SIN(obj(15, 3)))
obj(15, 8) = obj(13, 8) + (obj(15, 2) * SIN(obj(15, 4)))
Name$(18) = "FootR"
obj(18,1)=16: obj(18,2)=20: obj(18,3)=(0/57.3) +obj(16,3): obj(18,4)=(90/57.3) +obj(16, 4)
obj(18, 6) = obj(16, 6) + (obj(18, 2) * COS(obj(18, 4)) * COS(obj(18, 3)))
obj(18, 7) = obj(16, 7) + (obj(18, 2) * COS(obj(18, 4)) * SIN(obj(18, 3)))
obj(18, 8) = obj(16, 8) + (obj(18, 2) * SIN(obj(18, 4)))
Name$(19) = "FootL"
obj(19,1)=17: obj(19,2)=20: obj(19,3)=(0/57.3) +obj(17,3): obj(19,4)=(90/57.3) +obj(17, 4)
```

```
obj(19, 6) = obj(17, 6) + (obj(19, 2) * COS(obj(19, 4)) * COS(obj(19, 3)))
obj(19, 7) = obj(17, 7) + (obj(19, 2) * COS(obj(19, 4)) * SIN(obj(19, 3)))
obj(19, 8) = obj(17, 8) + (obj(19, 2) * SIN(obj(19, 4)))

'Draw Stick Man
For n = 2 To Nobjects
Line (obj(obj(n, 1), 6) + 200, obj(obj(n, 1), 7) + 50)-(obj(n, 6) + 200, obj(n, 7) + 50)
Next n
```

Chapter 7

Virtual applications

Virtual reality is a development of a number of previous technologies, including simulators, interactive multimedia systems, and computer and arcade games. Each of these areas offers applications for VR, and there are also a number of new emergent applications which are now practical.

This chapter looks at a range of virtual reality applications in training and education, entertainment, medicine, design and industry. In education and training virtual reality offers a low cost route to simulation, with applications ranging from teaching history in schools to military training. From medicine to industrial design, the use of 'virtual humans' is becoming widespread, and we look at several of these applications. In science and industry, virtual reality tools are being uses to aid visualisation in 3D, with applications ranging from modelling molecular structures to aircraft design.

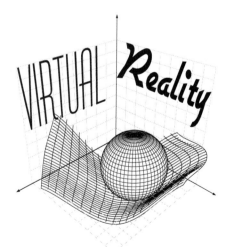

Training and education

One of the major building blocks of VR work was flight simulation. VR retains a lot in common with flight simulation and can provide a training environment in which mistakes are less permanent and costly than they would be in reality. Pilots and tank commanders trained today in complex simulators will in the near future be trained in VR. As VR can incorporate multiple participants, in competition or in combat with one or other, it is likely to find successful applications in many forms of combat training. In civilian training VR will be useful in allowing chemicals and machinery to be handled without physical danger to the users. Applications could include the management of nuclear power stations or chemical plants. VR will also provide a useful tool for education, supporting 'learning by doing'. Applications for teaching physics and chemistry are already being developed. Less obvious applications include allowing users to 'enter' a period of history.

Entertainment

Figure 7.1 The Virtuality® Entertainment System. Reproduced by kind permission of *Virtuality Entertainment Ltd*, Leicester, UK

Entertainment is another application area where VR is an extension of existing technologies, with cinema and video and computer games as precursors to VR. As the technology improves there will be a strong market for VR in home entertainment and arcade games. Two routes of development are likely: low tech, low cost VR for use in the home and high tech, high cost VR which is hired by the minute by large numbers of users.

Virtualtiy® systems are one example of the high-tech route, VR game systems originally developed for use in video arcades. The stand-up Virtualtiy system uses a Visette® head-mounted display and a hand-held pointing device to control movement of a virtual hand and weapon seen on the display. A number of different games may be played on this machine, including the famous Dactyl Nightmare – a hunt-and-shoot epic. A second sit-down Virtualtiy system offers more simulation-based games – such as car racing.

Medicine

Virtual reality technology is beginning to be used in various medical and health related areas. Due to the enormous complexity of the human anatomy the ability to generate complete virtual replicas of the human body is still many years away. However, a number of promising medical applications are appearing. One project in the USA is focusing on modelling the abdominal area. The aim is to develop both a teaching tool and a method of practising surgical procedures.

The virtual abdomen is cartoon-like due to current limits of computer power and display technology, but the simulation is realistic in its anatomical and technical accuracy and supports good interactivity with the model's internal organs. Instruments such as scalpels and clamps may be grasped and manipulated. Anatomical structures may be evaluated from any angle, giving new perspectives, and allowing medical students to study the digestive tract without actually performing surgery or dissecting a corpse.

Virtual humans

Many VR applications are being developed based on 'virtual humans', simulations of the human body. In the Department of Design at Brunel University, 3D human models are being used to investigate the mechanical interaction between users and industrial products.

Figure 7.2
Simulation of kettle pouring. Reproduced by permission of Gail Jeffries

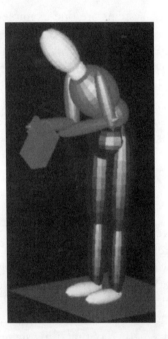

Eventually, human modelling may be used as a routine tool in the development of industrial products, shortening the prototyping stage of the design process. One case study at Brunel used the Adams Android, a 3D human model, to simulate and analyse the use of a kettle by a woman with rheumatoid arthritis of the wrist. Information on the forces and moments in the joints resulting from kettle use could be used to improve future kettle designs. Another study at Brunel uses a finite element model to investigate forces and their distributions in passenger restraint systems, (seatbelts, tensioners and airbags), and the human body. The focus is on modelling the behaviour of the human hip, and soft tissues in the abdomen, under crash conditions, to improve user comfort and safety.

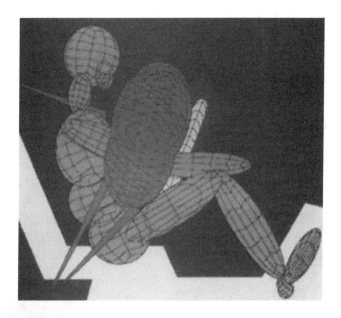

Figure 7.3
Modelling of
passenger
restraint
systems.
Reproduced by
permission of
Kai Leibrandt

Molecular modelling

Researchers at the University of York are working with a number of industrial collaborators to develop VR tools for molecular modelling. They hope eventually these tools will be used for the design of new drugs. Conventional molecular graphics systems permit scientists to manipulate molecular models, but representing 3D models on 2D screens with 2D mouse interfaces has limitations. In an immersive VR system with 3D mice, the chemist can hold the molecules in his hands, twist them, turn them, see how their shapes relate, as if the molecules were real, solid objects. This helps the chemist build a better understanding of the molecular structure.

Concept design

Researchers and students at Coventry School of Art and Design are using virtual reality to visualise their automotive designs in full size before mock-ups and scale models are built. The aim is to reduce the number of expensive concept design models which are built during the vehicle design cycle, and to eliminate design problems earlier in the process. They are trying to recreate the experience of standing next to a car, walking round it, opening doors and getting the 'feel' of the car design.

Kitchen design

Several companies are using VR systems to let customers see their new kitchen or bathroom before they buy it. In one system the customers bring a floor plan of their present kitchen to the showroom. They then specify the new units they wish to buy, and their preferred design is built into a VR model.

Figure 7.4
Bathroom
Design.
Reproduced by
permission of
British Gas plc

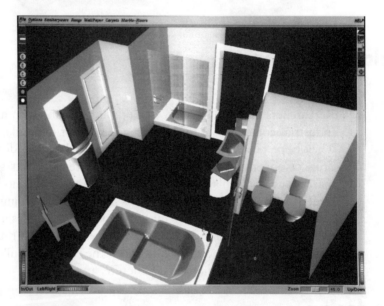

Virtual manufacturing

Researchers at the University of Bath are building a 'virtual workshop' to allow designers to 'make' components using realistic three-dimensional representations of machine tools. Mistakes will be able to be edited at the touch of a key, so virtual designers will be able to refine designs through trial and error without wasting real materials. The workshop is viewed by watching a computer screen through stereoscope liquid crystal glasses. The computer-simulated lathes and mills will work in the same way as their real counterparts and feature identical control panels.

Industrial applications

Industry is evaluating a number of possible applications. Where an engineer is trying to develop a mental image of a very complex collection of parts, sticking his head into the design and looking around should be more effective than merely looking at it 'through the window' of a workstation. VR systems should enable design faults to be ironed out without having to building physical prototypes of each possible design.

Applications being developed are as diverse as aircraft engine design, submarine compartment visualisation, environmental-impact studies, and nuclear repository design. One of the first demonstrators to get under way addresses the future potential for using VR to complement computer-aided design (CAD) activities in Rolls Royce's 'digital pre-assembly' department.

Physical mock-ups of aircraft engines – in this case the Trent 800 system for the Boeing 777 – can cost millions of pounds to build; yet it is during the fabrication process that some problems of maintainability become apparent. In particular, there are those problems that may arise from the limited abilities of conventional CAD workstations to provide their users with an 'intuitive' or natural view of the engine and its components. VR is being considered to offer a logical design step between Rolls Royce's CAD modelling activities and mock-up fabrication phases. 'Immersees' will experience the service layout of an engine, providing an early assessment of the planned distribution of services – pipework, gearboxes, brackets etc – for their ease of maintainability.

Datasuits and body recognition

Commercial systems exist which can recognise your body position and movement through space. VPL research developed a datasuit which used the same fibre-optic sensing technology as the dataglove to monitor 50 different joints on the body. The knees, arms and torso were sensed and four Polhemus sensors tracked heads, hands and the back. The suit was used for research into how humans move, and was also used by Hollywood computer animators. Researchers in the Media Lab at MIT have also produced a suit which can be used to program animation movement.

A bodysuit project

Using the same technology as the gloves in Chapter 2, a basic body recognition suit could be put together. The same sensor–LED pairs and circuits could be used, but this time the connecting plastic tubing would be extended to 0.5 m lengths. The tubing could be taped across the elbows and knee joints of some tight fitting clothing, then as you flex your arms and legs the voltages at the sensors would change. These sensor values could be used to animate the simple 'stick man' model of the human body we saw in the last section. With a little more work you could develop a dance or karate tutor!

A career in VR?

At present the number of jobs advertised each year in VR is very small. However, there is growing industry in the UK producing and distributing VR products and employing about 700 people. There does appear to be enormous potential for growth. Workers in VR come from a wide range of backgrounds, from computing to psychology, ergonomics and engineering. Skill requirements on the engineering and computing side include good knowledge of computer-aided design and computer graphics and good software skills. As much of VR is about perception, psychologists and ergonomists are vital team members. As VR technology improves design and visual skills will be of increasing importance for VR workers. Already designers creating virtual worlds, such as those seen on TV game shows, use virtual reality tools, and their backgrounds are more visual than technical.

Appendix A: manual for the dataglove software

To run the dataglove software, from DOS enter drive A and type CD\DATAGLOVE, from this directory type VR-NOGLOV. This will run the 'Noglove' version which will run without a glove connected, as a demonstration. If you have built a glove type VR'V5-31 from the dataglove directory, and this will run a version which is expecting voltage input from a glove. On starting up in VR'V5-31 the message window will prompt you to calibrate the glove. Once this is done you are free to move the hand. Press SPACE to start the pose recognition algorithm. The 'Noglove' version skips the calibrate routine.

Menu options

The Menus may be accessed by pressing the initial letter of that menu, then the highlighted letter of the function you want. The cursor keys can also be used. A brief help line is shown in the message window. The menus are described in the table below.

Command	Option	Meaning
File	Open	Opens an existing pose file from disk
	New	Creates a New, blank pose file
	Save	Save the current poses to disk
	Rename	Renames the current pose file
	DOS Shell	Temporarily exits to DOS
	Quit	Exits the program
Edit	Change	List the poses, then change one
	Add	Adds a new pose to the current file
	Delete	Deletes a pose from the file
	Show pose	Displays the hand in a pose
Options	Recalibrate	Enables you to recalibrate the glove

		3D Colours	Lets you change the 3D view colours
	View	Side	Change the view angle to side
		Front	Change the view angle to front
		User Angle	Enter the values for Spin and Tilt
		Wire Frame	Change the view to wire frame
		Solid Body	Change the view to solid
		Three-D	Change the view to 3D

The dataglove
software screen

Menu Bar   Menu   Display Window   Axes Window

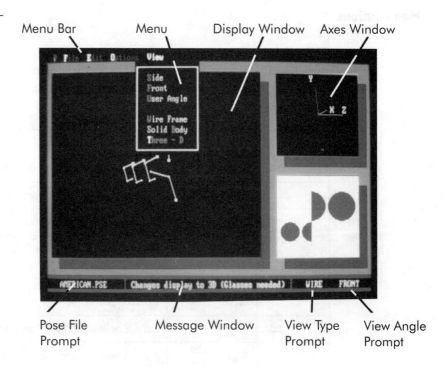

Pose File   Message Window   View Type   View Angle
Prompt   Prompt   Prompt

Software flowchart

The software
flowchart

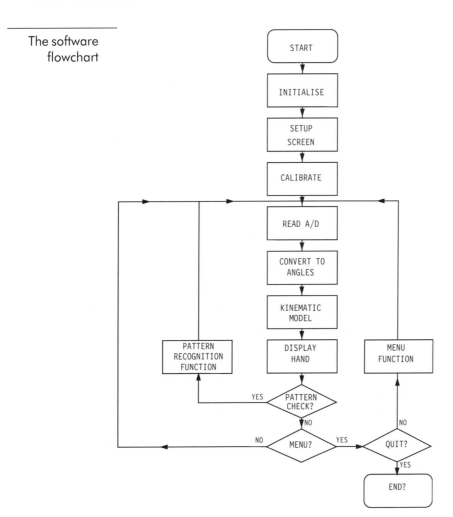

Appendix B: parts list for the dataglove

Sensors

- 5 small light-dependant resistors, from *Radio Spares*, part 596-141 (approximately 80 pence each).
- 5 narrow-beam LEDs (normal LEDs will work).
- Approximately 1 m of thin black-plastic tube. Note that the internal diameter of the tubing needs to be similar to the external diameter of your LEDs. One possible supplier is:

> *Hyphose Ltd*
> Unit 3, The Warrior Centre
> Fitzherbert Road
> Farlington, Portsmouth
> Tel: 01705 324644

Glove

- 1 black fabric glove and some black fabric tape.

Circuit

- 5 × 1.1 MΩ resistors.
- 5 × 150 Ω series resistors for the LEDs.
- Approximately 1 m of 20 wire ribbon cable.
- Various connectors, (25-pin D-type if using the *Roldec A/D* board).

Also required

- A/D convertor board, for PC. One possible supplier is:

> *Roldec Systems*
> Roldec House
> 504 Dudley Road
> Wolverhampton
> WV2 3AA
> Tel: 01902 456464

They have a 16-channel board for approximately £50.

- ▸ PC computer.
- ▸ 5 volt power supply.

Mechanical tracker

Sensors
- ▸ $3 \times 2.2\,M\Omega$ linear, single-turn, potentiometers.

Structure
- ▸ 3 balsa wood spars, dimensions of your choice.

Also required
- ▸ A/D convertor board, as above.
- ▸ Approximately 2 m of ribbon cable and 25-pin D-type connector to connect potentiometers to the A/D board.
- ▸ 5 volt power supply.

Template for 3D glasses

Use the template below to cut a piece of thin card in a 'glasses' shape. Get hold of two small pieces of plastic photographic filter, one red and one green, to stick over the right and left eyeholes. (You can buy this filter from photographic shops, but a keen photographer may have some offcuts). Try the glasses with the 3D rotating hand...

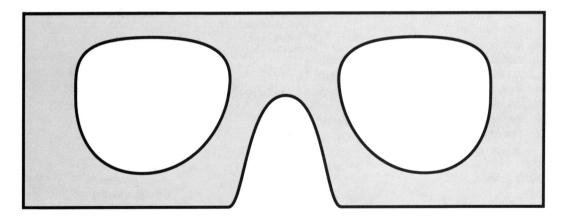

Index